D0931322

WITHDRAWN-UNL

The House and Home

A review of 900 years of House planning and furnishing in Britain

The House and Home

A review of 900 years of House planning and furnishing in Britain

M W Barley

New York Graphic Society Ltd.
Greenwich, Connecticut

Standard Book Number 8212–0351–7
Library of Congress Catalog Card Number 72–162716

© M. W. Barley 1963

First published in U.S.A. 1971 by
New York Graphic Society Ltd,
Greenwich, Connecticut

Printed in Great Britain by
The Anchor Press Ltd, Tiptree, Essex

NA
7328
.B24
1971

Contents

7   Author's Note

8   List of Figures

9   List of Illustrations

13   Introduction

20   The Later Middle Ages

31   The First Housing Revolution

47   The Rural House

56   The Town House

73   Notes

75   Bibliographical Notes

205   Index

To Diana

This book attempts, within a modest compass of text and pictures, to draw together the story of the house in this island within historic times. Text and illustrations run parallel to each other, and the principal thread is the needs and wishes of the family in different ages and in widely differing social and economic circumstances. Modern photographs have been used, rather than paintings or other contemporary illustrations, since the latter were made for other than record purposes and so fail, in one respect or another, to make historical points distinctly and accurately. The reader must be left to fill the rooms with people about their homely affairs.

In the search for illustrations I have had the help of the staff of the National Buildings Record in London and of the Scottish National Buildings Record (Ministry of Works) in Edinburgh; the Curator of the Welsh Folk Museum, St. Fagan's; the Director and staff of the School of Scottish Studies in the University of Edinburgh and the Editor of the Survey of London, London County Council; the Librarians of Chorley, Leeds and Nottingham; the Curators of the Manx Museum and of the Luton and Norwich Museums; the Archivist of the Flintshire County Record Office and the Librarian of the William Salt Library, Stafford; Dr. Margaret Wood; Messrs. Dennis Brough, A. W. Everett, S. R. Jones, W. Kissling, John Prest, P. S. Spokes and C. F. Stell. Dr. Patrick Nuttgens, Mr. G. D. Hay and Dr. P. L. Payne put their knowledge of Scotland at my disposal. Sir John Summerson and Mr. A. Oswald have allowed me to reproduce figures 4 and 8. Mr. N. Summers prepared most of the drawings for the introduction.

Professor Jack Simmons, the General Editor, has both spurred me on and guided my efforts; if the result fails to measure up to his concept, the shortcomings are mine.

M. W. B.

List of Figures

1 The elements of the later medieval house.

2 Plan of a Devonshire long house, Higher Grenofen, Whitchurch. (S. R. Jones)

3 Map of part of Great Yarmouth. (Society of Antiquaries of London)

4 Plan of Hardwick Hall, Derbyshire. (after B. Stallybrass, *Archaeologia* v. 64)

5 Plan and elevation of the Priory, Marcham, Berkshire. (E. M. Jope)

6 Plans of Claypotts Castle, Angus. (D. MacGibbon and T. Ross)

7 Plan of a West Riding clothier's house. (W. B. Trigg)

8 Plans of 'double piles': the Priory, Brant Broughton, Lincolnshire, and High House, Penrhos, Monmouthshire. (Routledge and Kegan Paul and the Trustees of the National Museum of Wales)

9 Plan of Eastbury Park, Dorset. (after Colen Campbell, *Vitruvius Britannicus*, 1725)

10 Plan and elevation of a house at Airth, Stirling. (Scottish N.B.R.)

11 Design for model farm labourer's cottage in Scotland, 1812. (Sir John Sinclair)

12 Plan of terrace houses in Alfred Street, Bath, 1772. (N.B.R.)

13 Plan of terrace houses in Zulu Road, Nottingham, 1879. (Corporation of Nottingham)

14 Farm labourers' cottages, Bletchingdon, Oxfordshire, 1796. (T. Rayson)

15 Design for weavers' tenements at Bannockburn, Stirling, 1780. (Trustees of the National Library of Scotland)

16 Elevation of weavers' tenements at New Lanark. (Scottish N.B.R.)

List of Illustrations

The author and the publishers wish to thank the Trustees of the National Library of Scotland for permission to reproduce the plan from the Wilson Collection on which figure 15 is based. The items marked R.C.H.M., R.C.A.H.M. and M.O.W. are supplied by the Royal Commission on Historical Monuments (England), the Royal Commission on Ancient and Historical Monuments (Wales) and the Ministry of Works respectively; those marked Scottish N.B.R. are supplied by the Scottish National Buildings Record, Ministry of Works. All these are reproduced by permission of the Controller of Her Majesty's Stationery Office. Item 26 is reproduced by permission of the Air Ministry, with Crown copyright reserved. Those marked N.B.R. are from the National Buildings Record.

1 First-floor hall in the Bayeux Tapestry.
2 Burford, Oxfordshire. (David Marsh, Antiques)
3 Little Wenham, Suffolk. (Hallam Ashley)
4 Cottages in the Bayeux Tapestry.
5 Link Farm, Egerton, Kent.
6 Great Dixter, Northiam, Sussex. (N.B.R.)
7 Monks Eleigh, Suffolk. (N.B.R.)
8 Treasurer's House, Martock, Somerset. (H. St. G. Gray)
9 Luddesdown Court, Kent. (M. E. Wood)
10 Misericord, Screveton Church, Nottinghamshire. (E. Richardson)
11 Winchester Castle hall. (Walter Scott, Bradford)
12 West Coker manor house, Somerset. (M. W. Barley)
13 Fir Tree Farm, Forncett St. Mary, Norfolk. (Hallam Ashley)
14 Alston Court, Nayland, Suffolk. (N.B.R.)
15 Preston Patrick Hall, Westmorland. (R.C.H.M.)
16 Church Farm, Parham, Suffolk. (N.B.R.)
17 Lavenham, Suffolk. (N.B.R.)
18 Woodsford Castle, Dorset. (P. S. Spokes)
19 Plas Newydd, Cefn, Denbighshire. (N.B.R.)

20 Vicars' Court, Lincoln. (M. W. Barley)
21 Longthorpe Tower, Northants. (F. W. Waters)
22 Haddon Hall, Derbyshire. (*Country Life*)
23 Dartington Hall, Devon. (M. W. Barley)
24 Glastonbury, Somerset. (N.B.R.)
25 Exminster Vicarage, Devon. (A. W. Everett)
26 Cotton, Suffolk. (Air Ministry; Crown copyright reserved)
27 Yardworthy, Chagford, Devon. (M. W. Barley)
28 Corbridge, Northumberland. (N.B.R.)
29 Affleck Castle, Angus. (M.O.W.)
30 Burneside Hall, Westmorland. (*Westmorland Gazette*)
31 Borthwick Castle, Midlothian. (M.O.W.)
32 Watton Priory, East Yorkshire. (*Country Life*)
33 Barrington Court, Somerset. (N.B.R.)
34 Otley, Suffolk. (N.B.R.)
35 Hergest Court, Kington, Hereford. (R.C.H.M.)
36 Preston Lodge, Cupar, Fife. (Scottish N.B.R.)
37 Gainsborough Old Hall, Lincolnshire. (N.B.R.)
38 Wollaton Hall, Nottingham. (Nottingham Public Libraries).

9

LIST OF ILLUSTRATIONS

39 Fyvie Castle, Aberdeen. (Scottish N.B.R.)
40 Claypotts, Angus. (M.O.W. Scotland)
41 Cranborne Manor, Dorset. (*Country Life*)
42 Cotehele, Cornwall. (N.B.R.)
43 Bartonbury, Down St. Mary, Devon (A. W. Everett)
44 Lacock, Wiltshire. (F. R. Winstone).
45 Preston Court, Glos. (S. Pitcher)
46 Madeley, Staffordshire. (William Salt Library)
47 Burton Agnes Hall, East Yorkshire. (N.B.R.)
48 Astley Hall, Chorley, Lancashire. (*Country Life*)
49 Thetford, Norfolk. (Hallam Ashley)
50 Stanton's Farm, Black Notley, Essex. (R.C.H.M., *Essex*)
51 Gray's Farm, Chignall, Essex. (R.C.H.M., *Essex*)
52 Bodidris, Llandegla, Denbigh. (N.B.R.)
53 Fir Tree Farm, Forncett St. Mary, Norfolk. (Hallam Ashley)
54 Maenan, Caernarvonshire. (R.C.A.H.M., *Caernarvon*)
55 Painted cloth. (Luton Museum)
56 West Stow, Suffolk. (N.B.R.)
57 Stamford, Lincolnshire. (N.B.R.)
58 Yaxley, Huntingdonshire. (N.B.R.)
59 Gladstone's Land, Lawnmarket, Edinburgh. (M.O.W.)
60 Rowarth, Derbyshire. (F. Thomas)
61 Tal-y-llyn, Llanbeulan, Anglesey. (R.C.A.H.M., *Anglesey*)
62 Cerig-y-Drudian, Denbigh. (N.B.R.)
63 Bryn-y-Ffanigl Isaf, Abergele, Denbigh. (N.B.R.)
64 Stow on the Wold, Gloucestershire. (M. W. Barley)
65 Brantingby, Leicestershire. (M. W. Barley)
66 Leverington, Cambridgeshire (M. W. Barley)
67 Monks Eleigh, Suffolk. (N.B.R.)
68 Ty Isaf, Hendre, Flint. (Flintshire Record Office)
69 Stickney, Lincolnshire. (M. W. Barley)
70 Hunt Street Farm, Crundale, Kent. (N.B.R.)
71 Raynham Hall, Norfolk. (A. F. Kersting)
72 Chirk Castle, Denbigh. (N.B.R.)
73 Cotton Hall, Denbigh. (N.B.R.)
74 Cawdor Castle, Nairn. (Scottish N.B.R.)
75 Kellie Castle, Fife (Scottish N.B.R.)
76 Elie, Fife. (Scottish N.B.R.)
77 Great Addington, Northamptonshire (N.B.R.)
78 White's Farm, S. Hart, S. Petherton, Somerset. (M. W. Barley)
79 Aynho, Northants. (N.B.R)
80 Chiddingfold, Kent. (B.B.C. Picture Library)
81 Stamford, Lincolnshire. (N.B.R.)
82 Hemps Green, Sibton, Suffolk (N.B.R.)
83 Baxter's House, Eaton Constantine, Salop. (N.B.R.)
84 Barrowby, Lincolnshire (M. W. Barley)
85 Almshouses, Brackley, Northants. (P. S. Spokes)
86 Sutton Bonington, Nottinghamshire (M. W. Barley)
87 Bulcote Manor, Nottinghamshire. (M. W. Barley)
88 Uppacott, Widecombe, Devon. (A. W. Everett)
89 Lower Tor, Widecombe, Devon. (A. W. Everett)
90 Thorverton, Devon. (A. W. Everett)
91 Tan-y-Craig, Llangynog, Montgomery. (N.B.R.)
92, 93 Yr Gegin Fawr, Pant Glas Uchaf, Caernarvon (G. Bernard Mason)
94 Bryn ffanigl Ganol, Abergele, Denbigh. (N.B.R.)
95 Jameston, Pembrokeshire. (N.B.R.)
96 Llaethwryd, Cerrig-y-Drudion, Denbigh. (N.B.R.)
97 Yorkshire hill farm. (B.B.C. Picture Library)
98 Royds Hall, Bradford, West Yorkshire (N.B.R.)
99 Scosthrop Manor, Airton, West Yorkshire (N.B.R.)
100 Horton Old Hall, Bradford, West Yorkshire. (N.B.R.)
101 High Bentley, Shelf, Halifax, West Yorkshire. (F. D. Montgomery)
102 Horton Old Hall, Bradford, West Yorkshire. (N.B.R.)
103 Coed y Cra Uchaf, Northop, Flint. (N.B.R.)
104 Grammar School, Burnsall, West Yorkshire. (N.B.R.)
105 Collinfield, Kendal, Westmorland. (*Westmorland Gazette*)
106 Pool Bank Farm, Crosthwaite, Westmorland. (N.B.R.)
107 Causeway Farm, Windermere, Westmorland. (*Westmorland Gazette*)
108 Clifton House, Queen Street, King's Lynn, Norfolk. (N.B.R.)

109 Lawnmarket, Edinburgh. (Scottish N.B.R.)

110 Chancery Lane, London. (B.B.C. Picture Library)

111 Great Casterton, Rutland. (M. W. Barley)

112 Aslockton, Nottinghamshire (M. W. Barley)

113 Stonesby, Leicestershire. (M. W. Barley)

114 Tydd St. Mary's, Lincolnshire. (M. W. Barley)

115 Holbeach Clough, Lincolnshire. (M. W. Barley)

116 Buckley, Flint. (N.B.R.)

117 Honington, Salop. (M. W. Barley)

118 Cilewent, Dyffryn Claerwen, Radnor (now in St. Fagan's, Cardiff). (National Museum of Wales, Welsh Folk Museum)

119 Drawwell Farm, Lyth, Westmorland. (*Westmorland Gazette*)

120 Bartonbury, Down St. Mary, Devon. (A. W. Everett)

121 Fulbeck, Lincolnshire. (M. W. Barley)

122 Widmerpool, Nottinghamshire. (M. W. Barley)

123 Cotton Hall, Denbighshire. (N.B.R.)

124 Llysan, Llanerfyl, Montgomery. (N.B.R.)

125 Bonshaw Tower, Dumfriesshire. (Scottish N.B.R.)

126 Underdown Farm, Eddington, Kent. (N.B.R.)

127 Bledington, Gloucestershire. (M. W. Barley)

128 Manor Farm, Steeple Aston, Oxfordshire. (N.B.R.)

129 Southwood Hall, Cottingham, East Yorkshire. (N.B.R.)

130 Key House, Falkland, Fife. (Scottish N.B.R.)

131 Cold Weather House, Nelson, Lancashire. (N.B.R.)

132 Winteringham, Lincolnshire. (*The Times*)

133 Offchurch Vicarage, Warwickshire. (N.B.R.)

134 Middle Street, Deal, Kent. (N.B.R.)

135 Blenheim Palace, Woodstock, Oxfordshire. (Aerofilms)

136 Syon House, Isleworth, Middlesex. (B. T. Batsford)

137 Houghton Hall, Norfolk. (N.B.R.: by courtesy of the Marquess of Cholmondeley)

138 Ditchley Park, Oxfordshire. (B. T. Batsford)

139 Osterley Park, Middlesex. (N.B.R.)

140 Easton Neston, Northamptonshire. (N.B.R.)

141 Stourhead, Wiltshire. (N.B.R.)

142 Melbury Sampford, Dorset. (R.C.H.M. *West Dorset*)

143 Durham Castle. (English Life Publications)

144 Invererne House, Moray. (Scottish N.B.R.)

145 Balnagowan Castle, Kildary, Ross. (Scottish N.B.R.)

146 Meadowfields, Whitby, North Yorkshire. (N.B.R.)

147 Corehouse, Lanark. (Scottish N.B.R.)

148 Old Cock Hotel, Halifax, West Yorkshire. (N.B.R.)

149 Cusworth Hall, West Yorkshire. (N.B.R.)

150 Fydell House, Boston, Lincolnshire. (M. W. Barley)

151 Offchurch Bury, Warwickshire. (N.B.R.)

152 Mamhead, Devon. (*Country Life*)

153 Mill House, Long Melford, Suffolk. (N.B.R.)

154 Toll House, Steanor Bottom Bar, Todmorden, West Yorkshire. (C. F. Stell).

155 Lock Cottage, Grindley Brook, Salop. (N.B.R.)

156 Newcastle-upon-Tyne (B.B.C. Picture Library).

157 Stamford, Lincolnshire. (C. H. Bear)

158 Stamford, Lincolnshire. (N.B.R.)

159 Walnut Walk, Lambeth. (L.C.C.)

160 Nevern Square, London. (M. W. Barley)

161 Scotch Street, Whitehaven, Cumberland. (N.B.R.)

162 Kensington Square, London. (N.B.R.)

163 Abbey Street, Bath. (N.B.R.)

164 Brock Street, Bath. (N.B.R.)

165 Mount Street, Liverpool. (N.B.R.)

166 Whitby, North Yorkshire. (N.B.R. (G. B. Wood))

167 Newark, Nottinghamshire. (M. W. Barley)

168 Whitby, North Yorkshire (Courtauld Institute)

169 London Road, Leek, Staffordshire. (J. M. Prest)

170 Hopping Hill, Milford, Derbyshire. (M. W. Barley)

171 Kilbarchan, Renfrew. (Scottish N.B.R.)

172 Blantyre, Lanark. (Scottish N.B.R.)

173 Shore Gate, Crail, Fife. (Scottish N.B.R.)

174 Inverary, Argyll. (Scottish N.B.R.)

LIST OF ILLUSTRATIONS

175 Harlaxton Manor, Lincolnshire. (M. W. Barley)

176 Kelham Hall, Nottinghamshire. (M. W. Barley)

177 Crawford Priory, Fife. (Scottish N.B.R.)

178 Goodrich Court, Herefordshire. (N.B.R.)

179 Balnagowan Castle, Kildary, Ross. (Scottish N.B.R.)

180 Victorian conservatory. (M. W. Barley)

181, 182 View and plan of model villa, 1808. (British Museum)

183 Ninetree Hill, Bristol. (M. W. Barley)

184 Kingston Road, Oxford. (P. S. Spokes)

185 City Road, Bristol. (M. W. Barley)

186 Clifton, Bristol. (M. W. Barley)

187 Lyme Regis, Dorset. (Reece Winstone)

188 The Old Palace, Oxford. (N.B.R.)

189 Tiptoft's Manor, Wimbish, Essex. (R.C.H.M., *Essex*)

190 Victorian family tea. (B.B.C. Picture Library)

191 Edwardian working class home. (B.B.C. Picture Library)

192 Edwardian working class home. (B.B.C. Picture Library)

193 Hayes Barton, East Budleigh, Devon. (A. W. Everett)

194 Edwardian working class bedroom. (B.B.C. Picture Library)

195 New Hall, Chirk, Denbigh. (N.B.R.)

196 Larder in early Victorian house (M. W. Barley)

197 East Kilbride, Lanark. (Scottish N.B.R.)

198 Stickney, Lincolnshire. (M. W. Barley)

199 Jurby, Isle of Man. (Manx Museum)

200 Ffynnon Goy Isaf, Llanychaer, Pembroke. (National Museum of Wales, Welsh Folk Museum)

201 Cottage, Somerleyton, Suffolk. (N.B.R.)

202 Ampthill, Bedfordshire (N.B.R.)

203 Sudbury, Derbyshire. (B.B.C. Picture Library)

204 Kiln Yard, Whitby. (N.B.R.)

205 Milford, Derbyshire. (M. W. Barley)

206 Llanidloes, Montgomery. (N.B.R.)

207 Nottingham. (M. W. Barley)

208 Stepney. (B.B.C. Picture Library)

209 Newark, Nottinghamshire. (M. W. Barley)

210, 211 Preston, Lancashire. (British Museum)

212 Stepney. (Dennis Brough)

213 St. Pancras. (B.B.C. Picture Library)

214 Leeds. (Leeds City Library)

215 Closet, Leeds. (Leeds City Library)

216 Kitchen, Leeds. (Leeds City Library)

217 Little Knowl Terrace, Todmorden, West Yorkshire. (C. R. Stell)

218 Newcastle-upon-Tyne. (B.B.C. Picture Library)

219 Broxburn, West Lothian. (Scottish N.B.R.)

220 Glenogle Road, Edinburgh. (Scottish N.B.R.)

221 Gorbals, Glasgow. (B.B.C. Picture Library)

222 Dewarton, Midlothian. (Scottish N.B.R.)

223 Rothes, Moray. (Scottish N.B.R.)

224 Macduff, Banff. (Scottish N.B.R.)

225 S. Uist, Outer Hebrides. (Werner Kissling)

226 Kentangaval, Barra, Inverness (Scottish N.B.R.)

227 Interior of Orkney house. (Leonard's, Kirkwall)

228 Interior of Shetland house. (Valentine's, Dundee)

229 Gorbals interior, Glasgow. (B.B.C. Picture Library)

230 Welsh interior, 1957. (R.B.C. Picture Library)

231 Boothtown, Halifax, West Yorkshire. (Bankside Museum, Halifax)

232 Faenol Fawr, Bodelwyddan, Flint. (N.B.R.)

233 Welwyn Garden City. (Welwyn Garden City Ltd.)

234 Council houses, Nottingham. (M. W. Barley)

235 Flatted villas, Corstorphine, Edinburgh. (Scottish N.B.R.)

236 Detached villas, Nottingham. (M. W. Barley)

237 Bathroom. (M. W. Barley)

238 Alton Estate, Wandsworth, London. (London County Council)

239 New tenements and cottages in the Scottish tradition, Dumfries. (Department of Health for Scotland)

Introduction

THERE ARE TWO WAYS of looking at the development of the house. One is to see it as the expression of man's technical and aesthetic ability in accomplishing a material end: the provision of shelter for his family. The other is to see it as the solution to a social problem, and to analyse the setting in which it is carried on and the conventions which govern it. The former approach inevitably emphasises the fluctuations in taste and style which buildings express and the technical skill of one age, or of one class, to the detriment of another. It leads, in fact, to injustice on the historian's part to whole periods of man's past, to whole regions and to whole classes in the community. This book attempts, both in these introductory pages and in the choice of the illustrations which follow, to describe houses as the expression of social needs.

To recite the factors which had their influence before ever a carpenter joined two pieces of timber together, or a mason laid one stone on another, will serve to indicate the complexity of what might seem a simple process. First of all, the vast majority of houses were, until the growth of the factory system in the last century or more, bases for the work of a livelihood as well as homes for the workers. The farmer stored and processed corn and milk either in the house or in the buildings essentially linked with it. The craftsman worked in one part of the house, stored raw material in another and sold the finished process from a third. The removal of the production processes from the house and its yard to a factory revolutionised the function of houses because it left them only part of their former scope. They became merely machines for living in. Agriculture was the last industry to be affected by this change, and farming still varies so much in scale and method, even within one county, that the revolution has not yet destroyed the evidence from which a lengthy past can be reconstructed. In our towns the houses and shops of earlier ages had much less chance of survival, and for that reason much less is known of them.

Throughout the centuries during which the house was a base for work, the relation between one house and another, in terms of siting, depended on the particular economic structure of a community. Few craftsmen had to leave the village or town in their search for raw materials—perhaps only the potter and the charcoal burner—because the processes of their craft required constant attention. They were therefore content to put up temporary dwellings of a very simple character. The mason, taken away from his home by a long building contract, put up a lodge which was house, workshop and office. For the rest, the journey to work was at most a matter of yards or a mile or two, depending on season and task. No one had to face a regular and irreducible journey until, from the seventeenth century onwards, both the urban and rural workers found themselves, in increasing numbers, employed for wages by farmers or industrial entrepreneurs.

From Neolithic times onwards the house has consisted of a set of rooms, or a group of distinct buildings, related to one another by function. The exception has always been the home of the family with no property or any responsibility other than for itself. Throughout the rest of society, the size and arrangement of the house depended on the numbers in the household and on its social standing. A study of local forms of the house in, say, the West Country and Yorkshire, can help to define the cultural differences between those regions. These variations have been little noticed by the historian and to a large extent they lie beyond his scope. They belong to the same field as other differences, such as whether bread and butter is put on the table already prepared, or whether it is cut and buttered by one parent or the other—a trivial matter, but part of the story of the family in a particular environment at a specific time.

A recent study of a working-class street in Liverpool[1] has shown that it consists of families which may embrace several households, for married daughters bring their husbands to the parents' home, and married sons like to live near their mothers. Such a revelation, that even in the second half of the twentieth century the house cannot always be equated with the family, ought to make the historian aware of threads in the fabric of society which his documents do not always reveal. The family, the basic element in the society whose history we wish to lay bare, may not always be the simple nuclear group of parents and immature children. There is ample evidence, of the kind that historians are used to handling, that in the earlier Middle Ages the larger family, which survives now in the slums of an industrial city and possibly in remote rural areas, was an economic as well as a social reality. It disintegrated by the thirteenth century among the peasantry, and had disappeared much earlier among the wealthier classes, but that it could survive a thousand years in a poor or a static society ought to provide a double inference. The first is that much writing on economic history, especially about small communities, may be vitiated by a failure to take into account ties of kinship which documents fail to reveal. The second is that the larger family, of three generations with mature children still under the parental roof, must have played a part in the early evolution of the house.

Although people who live in old houses very often make them out to be older than they are, many thousands do in fact live in houses built more than five centuries ago. No statistical count is possible, since the wealth of this island in ancient houses is as yet untold. Their antiquity may be impossible to discern from outside, or else visible only to the expert eye: suggested by the pitch of a roof, by a blocked window or by the ghost of a timber frame long since replaced by brick or cement. The earliest remains of domestic building—none of them now occupied as houses—go back to the later years of the twelfth century. The beginning of the story they incorporate is clearly much older still. House-building, a primary activity of man, already displayed the greatest diversity in different conditions. Apart from the evolution of the techniques involved, the domestic customs and arrangements which are embodied in it are tenacious in the extreme. Generation after generation of sons and daughters make their homes and bring up their children as their parents were wont to do.

The historian of architecture will be content with the view that the history of the house in Britain begins only with the Norman Conquest. That conclusion has one unquestionable element: that our cultural history is the consequence of conquest and immigration bringing to this remote island the crafts and customs, very often more advanced, of the continental mainland. Once established here, the blend of foreign and native shaped new forms of technical and social expression. But to think only of the most recent of a long succession of conquests is both inadequate and inaccurate. The art of building both in stone and in timber had reached this country in the third millennium before Christ, with the arrival of Neolithic farmers. The problems they had to solve in building their homes were not essentially different from those of the medieval peasant. We know little of the timber houses that such farming and pastoral communities were capable of building, but we can infer from less destructible houses of stone, built for instance in the Orkneys where no timber was to be had, that they could construct elaborate dwellings with all the built-in furniture—beds, cupboards, shelves and the like—that a simple life required. By the Iron Age at any rate peasant communities had their carpenters capable of making a joined and braced timber frame for a house or a cart.

It would be strange if some features of the house were not assignable to such a remote time as the Early Iron Age. The racial make-up of the island's population owed more to movements prior to and soon after the Roman conquest than to any other period. It would be too crude a view of history to credit any particular racial group with the invention of any distinct

15

form of house construction, but critical developments and the dissemination of new forms do seem to be the work of particular peoples in a particular environment. The evolution of the forms of house which were to be the basis of further development in Britain during the Middle Ages had already taken place before the Norman Conquest.

The one problem, to which a number of solutions had been found by the early Middle Ages, was to provide sufficient floor space under a single roof for a variety of needs, and in a reasonably convenient form: that is, as clear of obstructions as possible. The main obstructions were the supports required for a pitched roof. One solution, apparently evolved by the Germanic peoples of north-western Europe in the millennium before Christ and taken over from them both by the Celts and by the Scandinavians, was to support the roof on a double row of posts running the length of the building ⟨50⟩.* This had the twofold advantage of giving maximum width to the house and of providing a useful series of uniform bays in the aisles: it was one of the most fruitful elements in the ancestry of the medieval house. The aisled hall also gave the house-carpenter his grandest opportunities and his most severe technical problems. Another solution current among the Germanic peoples was to support the pitched roof on a single line of posts on the axis of the house. This seems originally to have found more favour in the northern half of this island, perhaps because standards of wealth were somewhat lower than in south-eastern England, where the aisled hall seems to have been the starting point for the upper classes. Since the axial row of posts was more inconvenient than the double row marking the lines of the aisles, it was superseded earlier. The axial posts could be shortened and their feet supported on tie-beams spanning the house from side wall to side wall.

A third solution, whose great antiquity is evident but cannot easily be substantiated, is the cruck method of building. Paired timbers placed at regular intervals on the line of the side walls are inclined together to support a ridge beam and hence the system of rafters ⟨44⟩. The method had the inherent advantage of not encumbering the floor space and, partly for that reason, lasted until modern times in the more remote parts of Britain. The suggestion that it may have come to Britain with the Celtic peoples seems best to fit the facts.[2] Its main disadvantage, of providing little head room, was in part overcome either by raising the feet of the crucks in the side walls or by choosing bowed rather than straight blades, but this method of building typifies the cultural relation of the highland and the lowland zones of Britain. The cruck building tradition of the highland zone was technically more primitive than other forms current in the

* The numbers in diamond brackets, e.g. ⟨50⟩, refer to the illustrations on page 77 onwards.

lowland zone, but it persisted, exemplified in houses of a very high order of craftsmanship and modified in detail, long after it was superseded in the lowlands.

Compared with modern housing these early homes seem remarkably large. There are as yet insufficient British examples to justify a generalisation, but on the Germanic mainland they were commonly 90 ft. or so in length, and 15 ft. to 18 ft. wide. No doubt such houses normally sheltered both a family—whatever its composition and numbers—and the family's livestock. On that assumption, for which there is a great deal of evidence, they are usually known as long houses. We shall have more to say later about long houses and their progeny in Britain. For those who wanted and could afford to build more than one barn-like structure of 100 ft. in length, the usual practice was to erect separate buildings. The barn-like hall had and retained until the later Middle Ages a communal or ceremonial quality. For special or more intimate needs, and for the elaborate needs of a great household such as that of the king, separate buildings were erected. One type—the small building with a floor sunk below ground level—has figured largely in the archaeological record of Anglo-Saxon dwellings in this country, simply because it is the most easily found. We are beginning to learn that here, as on the Continent, it was ancillary to large houses, used mainly as a workshop but perhaps also as a dwelling for the domestic servant or slave. The separate small building, used by women or by single men about a great household, is an essential element in the ancestry of the house and much interest lies in studying the degree to which the separate units are eventually integrated into a single convenient but complex structure. An account of a medieval house which omitted the secondary buildings would be as misleading as an estate agent's advertisement today which failed to mention a garage. Just as a modern house often has a garage under the main roof, rather than a shed in the garden, so one of the dominant threads in the complex weave of medieval and later development is the gradual emergence of a formal and organised pattern from the casual scattering of buildings about a yard ⟨22⟩. Precisely the same crystallisation of a coherent plan can be seen in the development of a medieval monastery—though the formal pattern was an import from France and not a native development—and of a medieval college at an English university.

One more element must be added to this catalogue of components: the storeyed building. Until the bungalow came into fashion—with a Hindu name to show that it had no connection with the labourer's cottage—the house of two storeys or more had for nearly five hundred years been thought superior to one with only a single storey. A Scottish reader will find it easy to grasp that this is largely a matter of local custom. Living in

B

flats, or on one floor of a tenement, became acceptable in modern times in those countries, such as France and Scotland, in which the tradition of the single-storey house had not been broken in the sixteenth and seventeenth centuries. Building a house on more than one level is of great antiquity in a mountainous country such as Switzerland. In this island subterranean construction, either for storage of foodstuffs or for defence, is equally ancient: witness the food-storage pits in corn-growing southern England in the first millennium before Christ and the souterrains of the highland zone. In Anglo-Saxon England the storeyed house emerges in two forms. One is the house built over an excavated cellar; the other is the house with living quarters on the first floor over a ground-floor cellar ⟨1⟩. The first has only come to light in a town—Oxford—in late Saxon times, before the Norman castle was built. First-floor hall houses of late Norman date to the fifteenth century still survive both in town and country. The principal motive behind such building must have been the need of the town merchant, or of the lord of a rural manor, for storage for merchandise or foodstuffs. Vaulted cellars, either completely or partly below ground level, are essentially an urban phenomenon of the Middle Ages because of the merchant's need for storage space on a restricted site ⟨2⟩. Throughout the Middle Ages and beyond, the countryman's cellar was on the ground floor, just a sin the medieval monastery the ground floor of the west range of the cloistral buildings often consisted of a great vaulted cellar.

It is thus certain that even before the Norman Conquest builders were capable of putting up a storeyed house if a client required it. Such building received a great impetus from the demands of new Norman landlords and the greater skill of the craftsmen who came in their train. Nevertheless, the most striking feature of the medieval house is that men of every class wanted the principal room, the hall, to be open to the roof ⟨6⟩. That is common to royal palaces, manor houses of every description and peasant houses throughout the country. The only exceptions so far observed are a number of stone parsonage houses in the West Country, which will be described later. It is not that parsons as a class were different, but that Somerset and Devon seem to have nourished a local tradition of storeyed building in the later Middle Ages which may have sprung from the first-floor hall. Parsonage houses elsewhere, such as the fine stone house at Market Deeping, Lincolnshire, or a small cruck-framed building at Morley in Derbyshire, show that the medieval parson's ideas about his house were no different from those of his parishioners.

The size and arrangement of the hall depended on the status and needs of the owner. At some point in the social scale came a division between those whose hall was used principally for formal and official occasions ⟨11⟩, such as meals for a large household, meetings of feudal lord with his military tenants or of the lord of a manor with his agricultural tenants, and the farmers whose hall was in constant use as a living room in which cooking was done, meals taken and a wide range of articles kept for every-day use. It is impossible to draw that line with perfect certainty, but it ought to leave most manor houses and larger houses on the one side, and most farmhouses and town houses on the other. Both types of hall were heated by a fire on an open hearth somewhere near the centre of the floor space. The open hearth was more convenient in the hall where large numbers of people assembled than in one where cooking had to be done, and for that reason it lasted longest—into the nineteenth century in fact—in the hall of a school like Winchester, or of an Oxford college. The peasant housewife preferred a hearth against a wall or partition to which bars and hooks could be fixed for her pots and pans.

Another development which overrides the distinction between what one may call the ceremonial, or official, and the purely domestic uses of the hall is the making of a passage through it, from one side to the other at one end ⟨13⟩. A stone wall or a wooden screen across the hall shut it off from the domestic traffic into the store or service rooms at the end; the official hall was thus less disturbed and the domestic hall was less draughty. This innovation belongs to the later Middle Ages, and the cross or through passage remained a standard feature of houses of all but the poorest peasants until the seventeenth century. The screens which make the passage in great houses or university colleges are very familiar, but the cross-passage in a Monmouthshire farmhouse of three rooms is of equal social significance, both from our historical point of view and in the eyes of the medieval householder. Bishops, barons or the fellows of a college built halls in which, apart from the windows and their tracery and glass, the eye of the beholder is drawn, and was always meant to be drawn, to the roof with its moulded beams and braces and to the screen. A country parson or a yeoman farmer was just as anxious to impress the visitor with those features of his house; although the ornament might be limited to chamfering along the edges of beams, the visual effect of soaring braces and panelled screen was just as carefully sought.

To the twentieth-century reader sitting in an upholstered chair with feet on a carpeted floor (and perhaps in a jerry-built house), there is a tremendous contrast between these elements of fine craftsmanship and display in the construction of a medieval hall and the lack of physical comfort for its occupants. Medieval furniture is very rarely to be found in our museums, and that is not just the effect of the passage of time. The earliest detailed inventories of medieval houses are from twelfth-century Essex, and they relate only to manor houses. They consisted of a collection of buildings of varying size and height, without any formal relation with each other. Where the contents are listed, the hall contained no more than a table, a settle and a stool or two. Just as in an early medieval church, seating round pier bases or along walls belongs to a time when the nave was not filled with benches, so in the medieval castle or manor house the carefully-made window seats imply a scarcity of other seating ⟨15⟩. In contrast with such simple furnishing the Essex manor houses had dozens of tubs, barrels, vats, troughs and other wooden utensils used for storing and processing food and drink. A somewhat later account of houses in and round Colchester, Essex, compiled for taxation purposes, implies that furniture was of little account at the end of the thirteenth century among farmers, merchants and craftsmen in a wealthy south-eastern county. Nine out of ten householders possessed homes with only one room. Most of them had no more possessions than the clothes they wore, and only a few had a bed and the essential cooking gear—a tripod to stand over the open fire, a gridiron for baking oat cakes or the like and a posnet or cauldron.

The Later Middle Ages

ALTHOUGH THE COLCHESTER INVENTORIES show so few signs of any comfort and convenience in the homes of ordinary folk, the aristocracy had by then begun to adopt standards and particular amenities which were to be a model for those lower in the social scale for the following three hundred years. There is a discernible rhythm in this aspect of social history, and one of its most marked phases lasts from the thirteenth to the seventeenth century in England, and into the eighteenth century or later in Scotland; by the end of the period, aristocratic innovations had reached the poorer classes. Another phase, one of whose aspects is the reception of Renaissance ideas in the field of domestic architecture, planning and decoration, began in the sixteenth century and had run its course only by the nineteenth.

Since medieval society gave so much of its thought to satisfying its religious needs and so much of its material resources to churches and other religious institutions, it is not surprising that some innovations in domestic life were in fact taken over from religious buildings. Glazed windows are first heard of in Saxon churches, though they were probably rare before the twelfth century. They are first indicated in royal palaces in a writ of Henry III. Their use spread through aristocratic and wealthy bourgeois circles during the later Middle Ages. In many houses glazing was only a device for admitting some light while the shutters had to be closed because of the weather; the upper half or less of each light of a window might be glazed, while the rest was shuttered ⟨15⟩. In a number of castles or manor houses it was not unknown for the glass, in its lattice of iron and lead, to be taken down when the household moved and stored for safety or carried to the next house to be occupied.

Paintings on plastered walls—either pictorial or a mere emphasising of mouldings and joints in masonry with bright colours—are known in churches of the twelfth century. They may well have been practised in houses of the same age, but began to be more widely done only from the thirteenth century onward. Similarly the art of embroidery was patronised principally for religious purposes—for vestments, frontals and the like— and then adopted for the house. A draughty medieval house was somewhat warmer with a curtain over the door, and an aisled hall more comfortable with curtains screening the nave from the aisles with their piles of bedding. Wooden benches were by the thirteenth century being made with a fixed back—that is, as settles—and they were more snug if they had a woven cloth or banker thrown over them, as well as a rush padding to the seat. By the fourteenth century such bankers often had a pictorial design, perhaps of a religious subject, woven into them. Cloth had to be hung round the bed, for true comfort; shuttered windows could scarcely be made draught-proof, and the design of the medieval house, as we shall see, meant inevitably that most rooms were also passages to other rooms. So the bed got its *tester*. These words of Norman-French origin—*chamber* for a private room, *tester* for bed curtaining, *banker*, *dosser* and *coster* for hangings for benches, chairs and walls—all show that the things themselves came into use while French was still the language of the classes who had them.

In 1253 an order was placed by Henry III for one thousand Norway boards to panel certain rooms at Windsor Castle. *Wainscotting*, as it was usually called, was no doubt intended mainly for warmth and to conceal the damp of stone walls. It became slowly more fashionable, and in regions where timber was plentiful spread eventually to the level of the country parson, but cost prevented its being widely adopted. Painted cloths were a cheap alternative to tapestry, but there was no such substitute for wood.

English custom had long required that one person should not be compelled to share a bench with others but should, on the most formal occasions at least, have a seat to himself—a chair. The word in medieval documents is the Latin *cathedra*, from which 'chair' is derived, and all the associated words and phrases—cathedral, in which a bishop's throne is placed, the university professor's chair, to 'take the chair' and so on—indicate the formal or ceremonial context in which the separate seat was required. It is in keeping, therefore, that the oldest surviving example should be the late thirteenth-century coronation chair in Westminster Abbey. A chair used for such an occasion had exceptional chances of survival; apart from it, medieval chairs can be studied now only in contemporary illustrations of one sort or another ⟨10⟩.

Let us now turn to the remaining items of furniture which became a standard feature of wealthier homes in the fourteenth and fifteenth centuries, and so set the pattern for the rest of the population of England in the sixteenth century. Medieval documents distinguish in the main two kinds of table. One consisted merely of planks laid on trestles; it was taken down between meals and laid out of the way, and was convenient for a hall where large numbers had to be fed, as in a magnate's house or a university college. The other was known as the dormant or fixed table. A compromise was the folding table, which was known early in the fifteenth century, and for occasional use the round table was already to be found. Forms, benches and stools provided seating, and were made more comfortable with cloth covers, and mats, hassocks or cushions. The medieval cupboard began literally as a board on which cups stood, but had become a formalised piece of furniture by the fifteenth century. Another type of cupboard, in which food was kept, was known as an aumbry. Some halls had moveable screens, either to stand across the entrance from the passage and check draughts, or to be used as a firescreen.

The furniture of the medieval sleeping chamber makes an even shorter list. Apart from the bed, which had a joined frame with a plank bottom on which the mattress lay, and posts for curtains, the chest for storing linen was the only other standard piece. But even on such a simple basis the house of, say, a fifteenth-century archbishop of York was splendidly furnished both in quantity and quality. Such men possessed a very large wardrobe, kept in a room of that name alongside the chamber. Since rich householders like these had so much linen, both domestic and personal, it is not surprising that the press had been invented by the early fifteenth century. Most of the furniture was made of native oak, but occasionally, especially in east-coast ports and their hinterland, tables and chests were made of spruce imported from the Baltic. Down to the sixteenth century 'Flanders chests', imported ready made, were quite common in upper- or middle-class homes.

In all these rich houses of the later Middle Ages there is a contrast between the simplicity of the basic elements, both in their design and in their fittings and furnishings, and the quality and scale of their provision. Wealth and ostentation found their only outlet in accumulating several expensive examples of a very limited range of items. The modern house, on the other hand, is filled with an infinitely greater variety of objects, fulfilling many specialised purposes, and of inferior craftsmanship. This

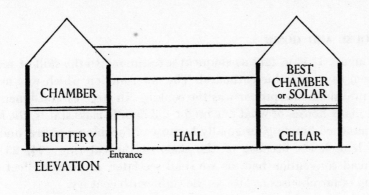

CHAMBER

BEST CHAMBER or SOLAR

BUTTERY

HALL

CELLAR

Entrance

ELEVATION

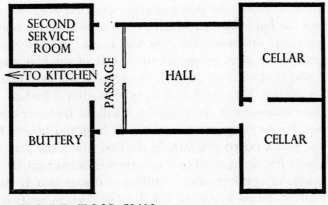

SECOND SERVICE ROOM

←TO KITCHEN

PASSAGE

HALL

CELLAR

BUTTERY

CELLAR

GROUND FLOOR PLAN

FIGURE 1. The elements of the later medieval house, shown in plan and section. The essential feature is the hall, open to the roof and flanked by storeyed ranges. Variations extended from a hall flanked by a single room to the arrangement shown here with two cross wings. Equally, rooms varied in size, their width being limited by the length of timber required to construct the roof trusses. By the end of the Middle Ages, the ground-floor room (or rooms) at one end of the hall was sometimes used as a parlour.

change began in the second phase to which we referred earlier, the sixteenth and seventeenth centuries.

So much for the standards set by kings and magnates and copied by the newly rich merchants. Now what of the houses? The expanding resources of all the land-owning classes led, in the twelfth and thirteenth centuries, to considerable diversity in house design, but by the fourteenth century their ideas had crystallised into what is commonly known as the typical medieval house. It has often been defined, in too limited terms, as a house of H plan ⟨see figure 1⟩. The essence of the plan was a central hall, flanked by whatever other accommodation the householder required or could afford ⟨7⟩. The design was well integrated and efficient, assuming that a wide range of functions was to be carried on under one roof and that personal privacy was no object. In origin it resulted from the drawing together into one structure of the separate buildings of an early medieval

23

manor house. It is in fact as eloquent a testimony to the skill of medieval craftsmen as is a Gothic cathedral. The one function which was not integrated into the house proper was the cooking. In large establishments, and even in many houses of what one might call middle-class status, the kitchen was a detached building, originally because of the danger of fire, and in the largest households because of the scale of the catering ⟨24, 25⟩. This widespread convention had, as we shall see later, a distinct effect on the planning of farmhouses as late as the eighteenth century.

How the secondary rooms were arranged in relation to the hall depended on their number; the one essential was that they should all be accessible from the hall, through which everyone entered the house. There is thus no essential difference between the house which formed a long rectangle, with one or more rooms on either side of the hall under a continuous roof, and that with wings at right angles to the hall, making an H plan. Every variation is to be found in later medieval houses. Entrance was by opposite doorways in the side of the hall, at its lower end, so that draughts from the doorways were minimised. In grand houses the upper end of the hall had a raised platform or dais on which the principal table was placed, both for social prestige—an urban merchant might have had one—and reasons of comfort, and its ultimate descendant is the wooden bench in a Scottish house known as the *deece* or *deas*. Sometimes the wall behind the dais was brought forward in a curved canopy, adding to the dignity of the high table and checking draughts round the backs of its occupants.

In contrast to this open hall, the remainder of the medieval house was, within limits which must later be defined, made up of storeyed building. On one or other side of the hall, or both, was a wing, roofed continuously with the hall ⟨8⟩ or at right angles to it, which contained a service room of some kind on the ground floor and another room over it. The purpose of this arrangement was not so much to double the accommodation as to get a room of superior status *upstairs*. It was commonly known by the Norman-French name of *great chamber* or *solar*; its open roof was made a decorative feature like that of the hall ⟨14⟩, and it often had a window of similar quality ⟨16⟩. Whether the room was at the dais end of the hall or at the lower end was ultimately a matter of indifference; the significant thing is that it had to be upstairs. The room or rooms below it might be known as the *cellar*, though its floor was not usually sunk below ground level. At the lower end of the hall there were often two rooms for drink and food known as the *buttery* and *pantry* respectively. The latter derives from the Norman-French word for bread, and the buttery from the butts or barrels of ale, *not* from butter. These names, solar, buttery and pantry, have got wide currency partly through the researches of Victorian antiquaries; medieval usage was less consistent. The main characteristic of these ground-floor rooms was that, prior to the fifteenth century, they were not used for anything but service purposes. This combination of a ground-floor hall with a first-floor best chamber, used apparently as a private bed-sitting room for the family, was the ideal for the medieval householder rich enough to have any choice. Neither historians nor archaeologists can yet demonstrate how two such elements originated and came to be combined, but the more peculiar, the first-floor chamber, must go back to a notion that safety in bed, without arms or armour, was to be found only in a building raised above the ground, perhaps with the ladder hauled up through the doorway or trap-door.

This type of house was to be found through most of England and Wales, but its distribution thinned out very distinctly towards the north and west. In parts of Kent and Sussex it was very common, in the particular form now known as the 'Wealden House' ⟨5⟩, among the middling peasantry of a wealthy region, but even that special design is to be seen in villages of the northern home counties and in towns as far afield as York, Stratford-on-Avon and Yeovil. In general, houses of equal size must have gone with households of equal real wealth, rather than equal status; the yeoman of Kent, as the Tudor verse teaches the schoolboy, claimed to be richer than the lord of a North Country manor. Even if the verse exaggerates the wealth of Kent, it is a useful reminder of the great contrast between economic standards on either side of a line from York to Gloucester.

The housing conditions of the lower ranks of rural society are still a matter of informed conjecture rather than solid evidence. The historian of architecture may be content to dismiss their homes as no more than hovels. The economic historian makes the more thoughtful comment that a two-roomed dwelling became the commonest minimum before the end of the Middle Ages. Can one go further than that? In the sixteenth and seventeenth centuries, when evidence becomes plentiful, we find that south of a line from King's Lynn to Shrewsbury the second room of a two-roomed dwelling was known as the *chamber*. North of that line it was invariably known as the *parlour*. Both words are Norman French in origin; they supplant the English word *bower*, which was current in Chaucer's time and lingered on in the recesses of the Lake District till Shakespeare's time. Both the new words in this context refer to the one sleeping room. 'Chamber' is certainly the older. 'Parlour' begins to appear in the four-teenth century; it is taken into domestic use from the medieval monastery, and it always indicates a ground-floor room. It spread to the Yorkshire gentry by the fifteenth century, and the word was taken into the Welsh language at the same time. If reliance on etymology is sound, it suggests that the poorer peasants of southern England acquired a second room for sleeping earlier than did their opposite numbers in the north midlands and beyond. These changes are not a matter of simple development and elaboration, or even of straightforward diffusion. A particular type of house, once well established in the popular esteem of a region, might last long after other types had got currency in other regions. The Wealden type certainly did so, even to details of construction such as the hipped roof with gables, or particular features such as the open hearth in the hall. The word 'chamber' having come into popular usage in the south between the twelfth and fourteenth centuries, lasted for three more centuries as the only word for a bedroom. The adoption of the name 'parlour' by the midlander took place at a time when a few rich farmers and gentry were making a momentous change in their houses. They ceased to use the ground-floor room at the superior end of the hall as a storeroom or workroom; they put in a fashionable fireplace, wainscotted the walls and ceiled it with moulded beams and joists ⟨52⟩. Though they called such a room a parlour, it usually contained a bed, and the absence of what we should call sitting-room furniture—chairs, or even stools and a small table—does not mean that they did not entertain guests there. The poorer peasants, without any such pretensions, simply used it as the principal bedroom for the master of the house and his wife.

Another profound change must have proceeded alongside this separation of the hall-living room from the sleeping room. That was the separation of the byre or cowhouse from the dwelling. This development cannot be observed from existing houses in the south-eastern half of England, but the evidence of the spade, and inferences from later records, both suggest that the long house was common in lowland as well as highland England during the Middle Ages (see figure 3). It had certainly disappeared from the lowlands by the sixteenth century. That is to say, the small farmer began to keep whatever livestock he possessed in a separate building for the short part of the year when it could not be out of doors. This left the family with a part of the house which had no special function. It was naturally taken over as a service room (that is, as a kitchen, buttery, dairy, brewhouse or just a general store) but variations in the names given to it and in usage show that as a service room it was a novel element in the late medieval house.

Things were quite otherwise in the highland zone of Britain. For climatic reasons peasant farmers were bound to a pastoral mode of farming, and united by an environment which offered few chances of taking in new land and enlarging the scale of farming. Neither Wales nor Scotland enjoyed the great economic expansion which transformed lowland England between the twelfth and the fifteenth centuries. In both countries, however, the native

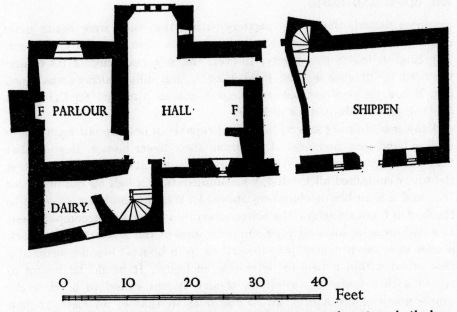

F PARLOUR HALL · F SHIPPEN

DAIRY·

0   10   20   30   40
Feet

FIGURE 2. Plan of a Devonshire farmhouse of the seventeenth century, in the long-house tradition: Higher Grenofen, Whitchurch, South Devon. House and shippen are built in an unbroken range, and from the cross passage one can enter the shippen under cover, though the cattle use a separate entrance. The room beyond the hall may have been a dairy originally, converted into a parlour when a new dairy (not shown) was added at the end of the house. This example is unusual in having two staircases, one in the usual position at the back of the hall, another to reach the chamber over the shippen.

aristocracy were in contact with English feudal traditions and the homes of the rich were transformed in the process.

Private castles sprang up in the twelfth and thirteenth centuries; some were built by feudal barons allowed to carve out whatever new territories they could in the Welsh border lands, or by Norman barons invited into Scotland by an anglicising king; others, both in Wales and Scotland, were built by native chieftains imitating superior ways or trying to provide for their families and their followers some security against new conditions of warfare. The castles of native origin were seldom as large as the English models on which they were based, but followed them remarkably closely. In the same fashion the lesser gentry adopted for their own needs a fortified type of homestead, which must have derived ultimately from the castle: namely, the tower house ⟨28⟩. From the fourteenth to the sixteenth centuries no northern landowner dared to live other than in a castle or a tower house, and it is worth remarking that in Ireland the same conditions produced precisely the same response; Limerick, a rich county, has no less than four hundred tower houses. Many English castles contained residential accommodation from the twelfth century onwards, and as the

27

centuries passed, the living quarters within the walls were made more ample and comfortable, but English conditions were essentially different. The English castle was rarely, if ever, the sole residence of its owner; the need for defence against local disorder and minor affrays was much less. Hence the contrast between English castles equipped for living and Scottish homes adapted for defence.

A tower containing several floors and capable of holding out against any raiding band was the essential feature of these tower houses. Beyond that they varied considerably. Where the risk of such attack seemed greatest the tower contained all the living accommodation: a hall on the first floor ⟨31⟩ and a chamber or chambers above. In Westmorland, less exposed to the fury of border warfare, the tower sometimes formed an accompaniment to a hall house of lowland type. On both sides of the Scottish border such houses were often called 'pele towers' or 'pele houses' because originally they stood within a pele or defensible enclosure. It would be wrong to regard such a house as primitive, though it was suited to a relatively simple mode of life equivalent in resources to that of an East Anglian yeoman. By the sixteenth century, at any rate, the windows were often glazed, the walls were painted or hung with cloths, and since the living rooms were entered only by a staircase they must have been snug enough.

On the Scottish side of the border these dwelling towers were often known as 'stone-houses', which indicates that the houses of the Scottish peasantry were timber-built, and more than one reference by English raiders shows that peasant houses were very easily demolished and re-built. For communal defence the border towns and villages built stone towers or 'bastels'; some villages had more than one and the town of Jedburgh had six. Since the houses must have been single-storey structures of very simple construction, none of medieval date have survived, and little has been learned about them from excavation. Many sites of medieval peasant homesteads have been located on the uplands of both Wales and Scotland, built on platforms on hillsides, the slope being levelled for the house; they were no doubt long houses, sheltering both family and live-stock, though some of the Scottish sites appear to contain round huts.

It would be wrong to suggest that the highland zone presented nothing but a contrast between castles or fortified houses and long houses. There is much evidence to show almost as great a variety in types of dwellings as in the lowlands. This was due to the essential characteristic of highland culture—its stubborn retention of ancient elements alongside a reception of some new features from the lowland zone. In the West Country this is shown by a few well-built stone houses of late medieval date, which have the best chamber over the hall. This, which might seem a very advanced feature, must in fact be a localised development from the Norman first-floor

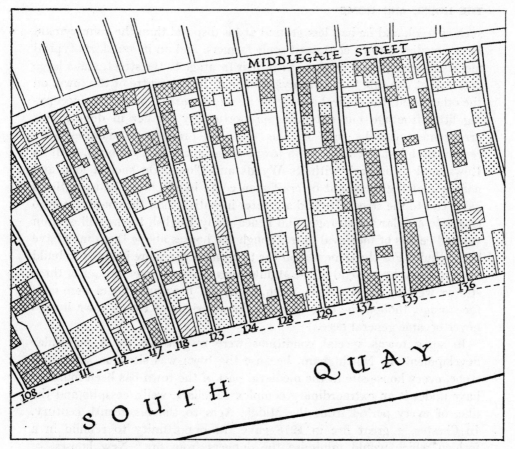

FIGURE 3. Map of the older part of Great Yarmouth, showing the common form of town properties in the Middle Ages: long narrow plots extending from one street to another or to a back lane. Originally each plot or tenement had a house at the front with a garden at the back, or a yard with stables, warehouses, etc. From the sixteenth century onwards these gardens began to be filled up ⟨167, 204⟩, and at Yarmouth this infilling took the form of rows of cottages at right angles to the principal streets. The houses hatched were built in the early seventeenth century, and those dotted by 1738.

hall. In Yorkshire, Lancashire and the Welsh border the aisled hall was an equally potent influence in the later Middle Ages on the design of manor houses and houses of similar status. The principal contrast between the highland and lowland zones is that while in the lowlands the house with a storeyed wing must have been a commonplace, in the highlands, apart from castles, fortified houses, manor houses and the homes of a few wealthy parsons or yeomen, not a storeyed building was to be seen.

No distinction has been made so far between rural and urban housing. From the fourteenth century onwards the influence of the special needs and conditions of the townsman began to have their effect. He wanted space under his roof for a retail shop, room for storing bulky raw materials

29

such as wool, and he had less ground at his disposal than the countryman. Every medieval town contained some farmers, and on its outskirts typical medieval houses could be seen, with their frontage to the street, and a large entrance at one side to the farmyard behind. In the centre of the town, on the other hand, the typical arrangement was of narrow properties, occupying little frontage but extending proportionally further in depth. This arrangement can be seen to this day—for property boundaries have remained almost unchanged—in towns as far apart as Yarmouth, with its Rows, and Edinburgh with its Wynds and Closes. On such a long and narrow plot the merchant or craftsman could build only a house with its gable end to the street. He had a greater incentive than the countryman to excavate a cellar for storage, and hence many English towns still contain vaulted cellars of medieval date, though the houses above them may have been rebuilt. For the same reason the townsman was more inclined to build upwards, and by the end of the Middle Ages timber-framed houses of three storeys were to be seen. Very often, no doubt, the upper floors were used for storage, though the outside hoist characteristic of Dutch town houses never became general here.

In some towns special conditions were responsible for a particular development. In Nottingham, because the town was sited on soft sandstone, every house site in the medieval part of the town has been found to have under it an extraordinary complex of cellars, wells, cesspits and the like, of every period from the Middle Ages to the nineteenth century. In Chester, a great fire in 1278 gave the opportunity to rebuild in a fashion which would minimise the dangers from fire.[5] New houses, of which at least twenty-five still exist in part, were built with raised footwalks above stone cellars; the footwalks were sheltered by the overhanging upper storeys, as was very much the fashion in French new towns of the thirteenth century ⟨The Town, 58⟩. Scottish town houses by the sixteenth century exhibited their own regional characteristics. The use of the ground floor for storage or workshop purposes was much more common here than in England, the staircase to the first floor being at least partly in the street ⟨173⟩. This design was no doubt taken over from England and France in the thirteenth and fourteenth centuries, at a time when the Scottish aristocracy were building castles and tower houses incorporating the same notion that the first floor was the principal living floor. Another feature of Scottish town houses by the sixteenth century was that they too had main walls of stone, because of the danger of fire, but they also had a sort of false front of timber, providing cover at ground-floor level for goods displayed, and a series of open galleries above. How common this arrangement was it is now impossible to say, but it must have survived from an earlier age of building in timber.

Before we leave what historians call the Middle Ages, something must be said of medieval sanitation. No one, however wealthy, enjoyed what is now regarded as essential to a reasonably comfortable home—a water supply piped to a wash basin or sink. The best medieval houses had a sink, commonly no more than a flat slab set in the wall at an angle ⟨18⟩, sloping outwards so that water poured on it fell down the outer face of the wall ⟨19⟩. A will made by a Yorkshireman in 1432 refers to 'a laver [jug] with a sinkstone, together with a brass basin'.[6] In some cases the basin had a metal stand, the jug hanging over it. These washing facilities were usually to be found either in the hall passage or in a sleeping chamber. Most families must have been content to use a wooden bowl or tub, and to empty the contents out of the back door.

The English have always been mealy-mouthed about sanitary arrangements, and many visitors to medieval castles are puzzled by seeing privies described as *garderobes*, especially as they have frequently been blocked or have lost their seats. Garderobe meant originally a storeroom, for clothes, armour and the like. At some time in the later Middle Ages the word parted company with the alternative version, *wardrobe*, and the older form was reserved for a closet with a stone or wooden seat over a chute ⟨20, 21⟩. Garderobes were always in upper rooms, never at ground-floor level; they were confined to upper-class houses with a solar, and were mainly for night use. Provision depended very much on the scale of the problem. A monastic institution had rows of seats in the reredorter; a medieval town like Conway might build a row of seats on the battlements of the town wall; the palace at Southwell of the Archbishops of York had three seats grouped round a shaft. In a medieval house of less than manor-house status a garderobe is remarkably rare. The countryman no doubt had chamber pots, and may have had a 'necessary house' or hut in the yard, but one is also reminded that 'in the humblest Irish farms it is customary for women to use the byre and men the stable'.[7] Such a practice must have been common in this island until recent times.

The First Housing Revolution

THE SIXTEENTH AND SEVENTEENTH CENTURIES are much the most important in the history of the house. The critical years were in fact 1575 to 1725. After that there was something of a lull in new building until about 1760. Then followed a second housing revolution which reshaped villages and gave many market towns a character they still possess. From 1870 onwards until after 1945 there was little new housing built in English villages or in towns dependent largely on agriculture. The great growth of population from about 1800 onwards, swelling old cities and creating many new, has left few traces of new houses of Tudor or Stuart date in larger centres of population. In any case, we are justified in dealing first with the countryside, since in early Tudor times only one provincial town had more than ten thousand people, and only twelve or fourteen others exceeded five thousand.

Growth in population was one of the principal reasons for the building activity of the years 1575 to 1725. Many country families must have migrated to towns; many that stayed had to put up with living in converted barns and stables, in large houses divided, or in cottages built overnight on the common land of the parish. Such dwellings must have been the rural slums of the time, and we cannot do more than note their existence. The growth in population went along with a marked economic expansion which eventually affected every part of the island, though in the more remote parts of the highland zone its impact arrived later and failed to reach the poorer levels of society. The scale of the expansion is difficult to measure, since there was, especially in the sixteenth century, a major degree of inflation. Primary producers found themselves with more money to spend, and a substantial part of it went, as in any inflationary period, into personal and domestic channels. There was much ostentation and display—'keeping up with the Joneses', whether it was Sir William Jones, kt., or Thomas Jones, yeoman—and domestic articles which had been a luxury became a necessity.

This great outburst of activity took place within an economic framework in which the building industry was still organised, with few exceptions, on a strictly local basis. The exceptions, though few in number, included the great houses which figure in the history of architecture, and those lesser, but still large, houses which reflected the ideas and ambitions of the aristocracy. They also included those buildings for which men of wealth were responsible, such as almshouses and schools. The other buildings of this period of nearly two centuries—farmhouses and the lesser houses in our towns—represent a fine flowering of regional cultures, in the materials used, the plan adopted and even the fittings and furniture. That these popular cultures were very much alive is shown by their ability to find new outlets in changing economic conditions. For one thing, the house carpenter found timber increasingly expensive; he used it more frugally and in eastern England made the best of a new situation by getting a plasterer to render the outside of his house in more or less ornate fashion ⟨82⟩. Elsewhere, the client eventually came to the conclusion that brick was cheaper than timber. A material that had been used only in eastern England, and then only for churches or great houses, came gradually into wider use, both socially and geographically: that is, it was to be seen in the east midlands a generation or so earlier than it appeared in the west midlands, and it was used for manor houses ⟨87⟩ and their outbuildings, such as dovecotes, long before it was used for farmhouses or cottages. The stone-mason held his own in these changing times with remarkable success. The first result of an increase in timber prices was the use of stone, if it was available reasonably near at hand, and many medieval timber houses were rebuilt in stone at this time ⟨44⟩.

Builders of every sort were subject to the increasing pressure of that self-conscious fashion comprised in the term 'Renaissance style'. How much they conceded depended on the client and his resources and expectations. The builder could put up a show of familiarity with new concepts in two ways: either by using, on façades or in interior decoration, motifs which were foreign and not derived from the Gothic tradition—strapwork ornament, or a pediment over an opening—or by giving his building a symmetrical elevation ⟨77⟩. The decorative features were of transient importance compared with the notion of a balanced appearance. The feeling for symmetry at first affected only the exterior, and while a brilliant designer like Robert Smythson could do it on a grand scale at Longleat or Hardwick (see figure 4), the small country builder could, for a long time, go no further than to arrange the windows of a gable end in symmetrical order, diminishing from ground floor to garret ⟨84⟩. The four-square design of Longleat, identical on each front, conceals a medieval type of arrangement, with open courtyards. By the middle of the seventeenth century the interior plan of such houses was symmetrical too. Larger farmhouses of 1700 in England often have the innate contradiction of Longleat, but before that century was much older the vernacular plan had disappeared; that is, the medieval tradition no longer determined its internal design. This was more than merely the submission of farmer and builder to an overwhelming fashion; it signified the disappearance, from the villages of lowland England, of a way of life based on kinship and community, and its replacement by one of farmers and labourers, employers and employed. We shall see this social change transforming the homes of the sixteenth and seventeenth centuries—first the great house and eventually the farmhouse.

It is perhaps a misnomer to call the great house a home, because it had always been an institution which also served as a home. It had to accommodate large numbers of retainers and servants, as one can still see at Dartington Hall, Devon, where the great courtyard is flanked by ranges of small rooms ⟨23⟩. Some great houses of the fifteenth century, still castles

C

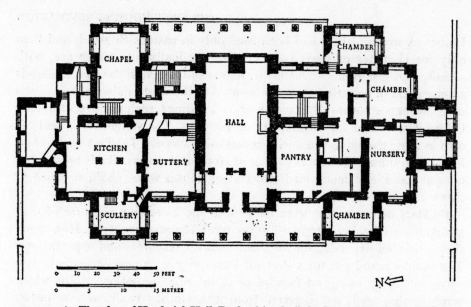

FIGURE 4. The plan of Hardwick Hall, Derbyshire, built by Bess of Hardwick 1590–97. In it Robert Smythson has modified medieval tradition, but has not abandoned it. The hall is still the principal ground-floor room, but here it is placed on the opposite axis from the usual. The service rooms are still at one side of the main entrance—two kitchens, a scullery, a pastry and a larder (on left). Various members of the family, such as one of Bess of Hardwick's sons by her first marriage and a nephew, had chambers on the ground floor, though the principal chambers were upstairs. (Reproduced from *Architecture in Britain 1530–1830*, Penguin Books.)

rather than houses, reflected a desire to put a physical barrier between the lord, his family and their personal entourage on the one hand and the large band of paid retainers on the other. By the sixteenth century strong government had altered the character of that dependent band but had not eliminated it. Layer Marney, Essex, a great house of Henry VIII's time, is well known for its striking gatehouse with eight-storeyed turrets; for our purpose its most interesting feature is the gatehouse which contained thirty-nine chambers, certainly intended for servants, while others slept over the stables in a dormitory. In Elizabeth's reign a new motive emerged for building on a grand scale: the desire to have a house worthy to receive the queen, and capable of accommodating the enormous number of courtiers and others in her train. Hence houses like Audley End or Kirby Hall contain not only splendid state rooms, but also ranges of bed-sitting rooms (as we would call them now) used by visitors on special occasions and for servants in the ordinary course. Another innovation which sprang from the same source was the long gallery, because it was an admirable place for a concourse on the occasion of a royal visit, or when entertaining the neighbourhood ⟨48⟩. In between times it tended to be used as a store; it was not always the dignified place which Nash's Victorian drawings suggest.

34

In the Elizabethan great house the hall was no more than an impressive lobby ⟨47⟩, except on formal occasions. The house was required to shelter a large number of people: the family, the household officers (of gentle birth, following feudal tradition) and a great number of servants. The family and its intimates required several private rooms, and familiar names came into common use—the withdrawing room, the dining parlour, or (later) the dining room, and the billiard room. Even in the south of England some of these additional ground-floor rooms were used as sleeping chambers, or as private bed-sitting rooms, but in the north midlands and the north this practice was much more common, and a great house there might have four or more parlours. As the aristocratic family came to need more rooms for private or state purposes, the demand for bedchambers also grew. Houses of two or even three floors, always with garrets in the roof, became a commonplace, and with that design there necessarily went more convenient staircases ⟨33⟩. The medieval newel or spiral stair, whether it turned in a narrow or a wide circle, was positively inconvenient. Framed staircases, with treads of uniform width and providing support on both sides, appear in the great houses of the Elizabethan age ⟨35, 36⟩. Some were placed, following the medieval tradition, in the re-entrant angle between hall and wing; others were placed in the central body of the house, taking up in effect some of the hall space.

In the great houses of early Tudor times, such as Hengrave Hall, Suffolk, the medieval plan was adopted of disposing the service rooms in a wing adjacent to a second court, the kitchen court. This design did not completely disappear in the following period, but in somewhat smaller houses a new and ingenious way was found of making a commodious but compact plan. Service rooms were put in the basement ⟨38, 71⟩. This development is passed over without special remark by historians of architecture, but this small innovation in a few great houses widened out until it eventually became the pattern of domestic life in a very large segment of Victorian England. For the servants, three or even four flights of 'backstairs'—narrower, steeper, darker—separated the dark basement where they worked from their equally dark bedrooms in the garrets ⟨72, 73⟩.

Below the great houses in social status came those of the gentry; houses which, for want of a more precise term, we may call manor houses. Prior to the eighteenth century, very few large houses in the countryside were not also the headquarters of a rural estate. The manor houses of the sixteenth and seventeenth centuries were the homes of men of very varied origin and status: lesser members of ancient and aristocratic families; the numerous members of the country gentry; men who had made a fortune in trade and bought a country estate, and also men of yeoman stock who had prospered in the favourable conditions of Tudor England. They were farmhouses, for agriculture was carried on from them, but the income of their owners came from rents as well as from the profits of farming. In the seventeenth century some landowners of this class became wealthy enough to build themselves houses which, like those of the aristocracy, were not surrounded by the mud and smell of the farm; then their bailiffs moved into the old houses, which were known henceforth as manor farms or hall farms.

Although manor houses form such a varied class, their development in this age of rebuilding followed a recognisable pattern. Ideas about the common E-plan as a compliment to a great queen are modern fancies. The significant facts about the design of a new English or Welsh manor house in this age are, first, that it adhered to the medieval tradition of a central hall, and second, that it was of at least two storeys throughout ⟨83⟩. Whether it had one cross wing or two depended on its status, and on the tradition of the region where it lay. The wings were no longer separated by a hall open to the roof. A medieval house could easily be modernised by having a chamber inserted over the hall; since height was limited, that chamber could often have only a dormer window ⟨50⟩. This improvement entailed building a fireplace in the hall (if it did not already possess one) and a chimney stack; whereabouts it was placed depended on local tradition and materials, and on the date at which the improvement was done. The one novel and very economical development of this age was to put the fireplace (or two back to back) on the axis of the house (see figure 5), so that the stack broke through the roof at the ridge ⟨86⟩. In a storeyed wing four flues could be accommodated in one stack, and this admirable idea, which probably originated in London in mid-Tudor times, had spread to Wales by the end of the seventeenth century, and, as we shall see, to the level of the small farmhouse.

What has been said so far of manor houses applies particularly to the south-eastern half of England. Elsewhere, marked regional variations indicate the persistence of a local tradition. In the limestone belt of England, especially at its southern end, the tradition of the medieval hall and cross-wing house, fully integrated, was not so strong. There one may find wings added or gables built up in ways which do not add to the formal and balanced plans and elevations fashionable in the south-east. The same is true among the timber houses of the west and north-west midlands, where the black-and-white effect of the native style had now its most elaborate expression. In the West Country the vogue for a courtyard plan, fully enclosed by domestic and farm buildings, extended much further down the social scale than elsewhere. In the counties on the English side of the Scottish border medieval tower houses were not abandoned, but an increasing number of the northern gentry built alongside them halls, service rooms and chambers in the southern tradition. On the other side of the

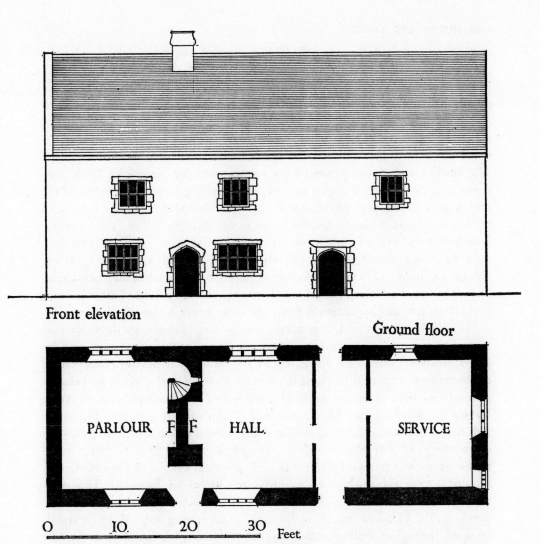

Front elevation

Ground floor

PARLOUR F F HALL. SERVICE

0   10   20   30   Feet

FIGURE 5. Plan of the Priory, Marcham, Berkshire. It is not in fact a monastic building, but a new house built in Elizabeth I's reign, and containing both old and new elements in its design. The ground floor has the traditional hall in the centre, with a through passage giving access to the hall and to the unheated service room; the third room would be called a parlour and used in part as a sitting room, in part as a sleeping room. The new elements are, first, that the house is of two storeys throughout, and not merely at the ends; second, that the hall and the parlour are heated by fireplaces back to back, with their chimney stack on the axis of the house; third, that there is an entrance in a novel position, into a small lobby by the side of the fireplace, giving access to the parlour and the upper end of the hall; fourth, that the staircase is in the parlour. There must have been a ladder from the service room to the servants' chamber or store chamber above.

border, however, the medieval tradition was elaborated, not modified. More space was required but, in the eyes of the Scottish aristocracy, had to be provided either within a courtyard ⟨74⟩ which was still more like a castle than the contemporary English courtyard (intended solely to set off the house), or else it had to be in the form of a larger tower house ⟨39⟩. Far more tower houses were built between 1560 and 1700 than in the preceding century and a half[8]. Instead of having only a hall on the first floor and a chamber or two above, smaller towers were built at one or more corners of the main hall-tower (see figure 6), so as to provide a more spacious staircase, still usually of spiral design, and more chambers ⟨40⟩. The tradition that the ground-floor rooms were for service or farm purposes only remained as strong as ever; the dwelling rooms were on the first and higher floors, and particular features of the plan, such as means of access from one floor to another, hinge on that fact ⟨75, 76⟩. French influence was certainly at work on 'Scottish baronial' architecture, but only to adorn and reinforce the strong native tradition. The Scottish nobleman clung to his castle-like house partly out of a necessary prudence, but more out of a feeling that it was a proper home for a man of his standing; its battlements distinguished it from the mere tower house of a lesser laird.

Within the houses of the gentry, fittings and furnishings developed in step with elaboration of design. Where lime or gypsum was cheap, smooth floors, both upstairs and down, could be made with plaster. Flagged or cobbled floors were still the best for service rooms. Glazed windows became general and were fitted permanently, instead of being removable. Scottish houses usually had only the upper half of the windows glazed, the lower half below the transom being shuttered; it is hard to know whether reasons of economy, or warmth, or safety were predominant. Wainscotting made rooms seem warmer and drier ⟨41⟩. Tapestries were still imported, and factories were established to manufacture them in England. Draughts through the doorway of a parlour could be checked by building an inner porch ⟨42⟩. Window curtains became a commonplace. Much warmth escaped through a ceiling which had above it only a boarded floor, and mainly for that reason plastered ceilings came into fashion, but an urge for display transformed the merely useful into the ornate. Ideas of comfort and display cannot in the last resort be separated and assessed. Painting on wall plaster was popular in yeomen's houses and the like in south-eastern England ⟨56⟩, and on ceiling beams in the great houses of Scotland ⟨59⟩. In sixteenth-century England there was a great vogue in farmhouses and cottages for painted cloths ⟨55⟩. They consisted of canvas stretched on a wooden frame, and fixed to the walls. The wall-paper which first appeared soon after 1660 was at first fixed in precisely the same fashion—pasted to canvas stretched on a wooden frame.

As for furniture, the various types already devised in the Middle Ages became more plentiful, more ornate, more comfortable. The great house now had chairs by the dozen, with upholstered and embroidered seats.

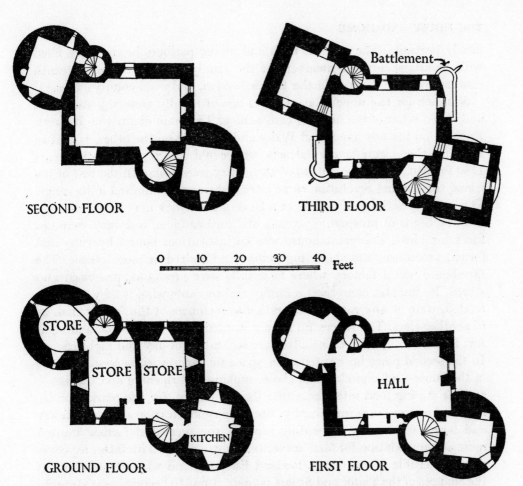

SECOND FLOOR

THIRD FLOOR

Battlement

0   10   20   30   40   Feet

STORE

STORE   STORE

KITCHEN

GROUND FLOOR

HALL

FIRST FLOOR

FIGURE 6. Plans of the four floors of Claypotts Castle, near Dundee, a Scottish tower house built in 1569. This type of plan, with round towers attached to opposite corners of the main tower, was very popular in Scotland at this time, because it provided additional chambers on each floor, making in this case two at the hall level (first floor) and three in all on each of the upper floors. The fantastic change from round to square form at the top of the corner towers can be appreciated by comparing plate ⟨40⟩. The house could be defended against marauders from gun ports at ground-floor level (one of them in the kitchen fireplace) and from the battlements at third-floor level.

The long table in the hall or the dining parlour became longer, and rested on a frame with turned legs rather than on trestles. The cupboard on which silver or pewter was displayed had to be larger, for pewter was bought by the set or 'garnish'. The wood turner and carver lavished their skill on staircases, panelling, tables, chairs, cupboards and bedsteads, and the joiner flourished under the demand for 'joined' furniture. While so many of these features of the Elizabethan and early Stuart great houses grew directly out of medieval fashions, one entirely novel aspect of the pride of family and position among the upper classes was the desire for

39

family portraits. The walls of halls and dining parlours began to be filled with paintings, first of members of the family and, in the seventeenth century, with landscapes in the Dutch fashion, and even county maps.

So much for the upper classes in an age of rapidly changing standards and ideas. What of the farming community? The main distinction between England on the one hand, and Wales and Scotland on the other, is that in England there were many farmers who could afford, during the years 1580 to 1640, to take note of what the gentry were doing. In the rest of the island the housing revolution came later and was more limited in its range. The building activity of a Cecil or a Bess of Hardwick may have put ideas into the heads of prospering yeomen and husbandmen, but they were not the same ideas. The great house was an institution, bound by rules and formal procedure, and sheltering perhaps a hundred or more people. The farmhouse was a factory where foodstuffs were produced, processed and stored. Its inmates comprised a family and servants who, if they were not related, were at any rate treated rather as members of the family than as of another class. The successful farmer wanted, first, more room and comfort for his family, and especially more separation of day and night rooms. In the second place he wanted more space for farm work necessarily done in the house—milk production, cheese making and ripening and the like— and for storing food intended either for the family, for the market or for eventual use on the farm. Thirdly, since the concentration of land in fewer and larger farms was proceeding rapidly, the successful farmer wanted more accommodation for farm servants living in ⟨127⟩. This latter aspect is most noticeable after 1660 in lowland England, and while it grew out of the changes of the Tudor and Stuart periods, it was to become most strongly characteristic of farmhouses of the eighteenth and nineteenth centuries.

The first consequence of this new economic and social climate was that in lowland England, by the end of the seventeenth century, houses having only one storey, even in part, were a rarity ⟨50, 100⟩. A few owners of medieval houses with open halls declined to move with the times. Poor labourers, such as the men who were compelled by the housing shortage to build themselves shacks on common land, lacked the means or the skill to put up more than a single-storey cottage of perhaps two rooms. The growing number of aged poor for whom villages found themselves forced to accept responsibility were given at most two rooms, either in 'poor houses' built specially for the purpose, or in privately endowed almshouses. The scale of priorities can be seen best by taking the labourer's cottage first and moving up the social scale. A separate sleeping room— called a chamber in the south of England and a parlour in the midlands— became the decent minimum of the labouring class by 1640. By the end of the seventeenth century that standard had been surpassed, and such people usually had a third room as well. It was not called the kitchen, for the living room, the only room with a fire, was and continued to be the place for cooking. Most people called it the buttery; that upper-class name became remarkably popular in all classes. On the question where cooking could best be done, the farming community was divided. For most the hall was the best place ⟨119⟩, and the service room was called buttery, milk-house, dairy or backhouse. Some farmers, and not only the richest, had a kitchen, and there were medieval precedents for turning the service room across the passage to that purpose, but the medieval tradition of the kitchen as a detached building, across the yard at the rear, died very hard ⟨25⟩. Many of the new kitchens were used only for brewing ale and baking bread, and they were tacked on to the end of the house as a single storey structure, or with only a loft over, suitable for farm servants to sleep in. Those who could afford a fourth room normally made it by chambering over one or more of the ground-floor rooms, and used it both for storage and for sleeping. It is at this point that the household ways of the gentry and of farming folk parted company. Everyone below the level of the gentry—parsons, farmers, craftsmen and labourers—had an interest in the land and so possessed livestock, had foodstuffs or seed to house and raw materials to collect or store. The rich farmer had special rooms, both in the house and in outbuildings: the cheese chamber, the apple chamber, the corn loft. Those with small houses had to be content to pile the sacks of corn or hang the cheeses in rooms also used for sleeping. By the end of the seventeenth century houses with the whole range of ground-floor rooms chambered over, providing at least two or three chambers, must have been the standard type for all but the village labourer. More accommodation could be got only by building a wing or two at right angles to the main range, and this the richest farmers did.

The planning of the whole range of the remarkable variety of new farmhouses which sprang up in this age stemmed from medieval tradition. They were one room deep, except for minor subdivisions such as a buttery taken out of a hall. The only significant exception is in northern English houses, where the medieval tradition of the aisled hall persisted in the seventeenth century in houses with a continuous range of offshoots at the rear, and this in its turn led by 1700 or so to new farmhouses being built on a square plan, two rooms deep. The hall-living room remained the focus of the plan, and the entrance gave onto it, except in those regions, such as the West Country, Wales and the north, where the medieval through passage was still popular ⟨78⟩. Only the most pretentious farmers had begun to use the parlour as a sitting room; for the rest it was still the best bedroom. Within the hall the relation of fireplace to entrance (the principal source of draughts now that windows were normally glazed) was designed

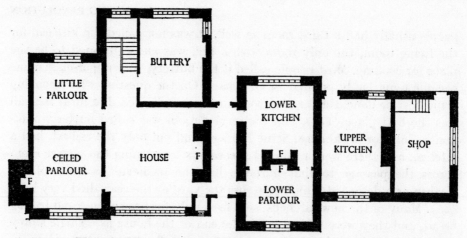

FIGURE 7. Plan of a West Riding clothier's house of the seventeenth century, based on Shibden Hall, Halifax. The design, with its cross passage, central hall and wings, belongs essentially to the medieval tradition; the hall fireplace backs on the passage, as is usual in the highland zone. The two modifications common in the West Riding at this particular period were the addition of a service room behind the hall, and the placing of one of the three parlours in the lower or service wing. The shop held the looms and other gear used in cloth making. The chambers upstairs corresponded with rooms below, except that a chamber for smoking bacon had in this house been made round the hall chimney stack.

to keep the hearth area cosy and intimate ⟨95, 96⟩. There the family could be warm, and could see the outer world through the small fire window without being seen ⟨90⟩. Whatever the standing of the house, the entrance was designed as a baffle. Small houses with two main rooms were planned with a chimney stack in the centre of the house containing two fireplaces, for hall and parlour, back to back; an entrance lobby provided the only communication between the two rooms, for the staircase filled the space at the other side of the stack.

Although the farmhouses and cottages of the whole island represented a final flowering of the quite simple medieval house design, their variety, both in details of design and in the use of materials and in furnishings, reflects the vitality of popular culture. Regional characteristics have begun to be exposed by local studies, but many counties still await close examination. In the West Country the storeyed house caught on rapidly, and stands apart from the south-eastern tradition; the chamber over the hall, instead of being the latest element in the design and so very often used only as a storeroom, was the best sleeping room ⟨88⟩; the parlour (that is, a principal sleeping room downstairs) was less important. In the north of England, however, the single-storey tradition was much more tenacious; as additional sleeping rooms were needed, they were added to the ground-floor plan, and called parlours, so that a Yorkshire farmhouse of the seventeenth century might have had three or even more parlours (see figure 7).

42

That involved using the service end of the medieval plan for sleeping purposes. In Westmorland, the only northern county of England which has been intensively studied, small farmers were very active in the period 1660 to 1725 ⟨107⟩. New houses, when owners were rich enough to afford a three-roomed plan, had a through passage and a staircase built out from the rear wall; small service rooms, if needed, were built at the back as outbuildings. The hall fireplace invariably backed onto the passage, so that access to it was as sheltered as possible. This arrangement is indeed usual throughout England from the limestone belt north and west, whatever the local building material. At a time when such farmers elsewhere had given up having internal partitions of moulded woodwork, and had to be content with stone, brick or cob, the Westmorland smallholder (for he was no more than that by modern standards) still had them built. Devoted craftsmanship went into the great cupboard built into the partition between hall and parlour, or the spice cupboard by the fire. In Scotland such built-in furniture was known as a 'breast of plenishing'.

How the village craftsman managed his work depended on the scale of his activities, the bulk of his raw materials, etc. Wool could easily be stored in an upstairs chamber; so could willow rods for basket making,

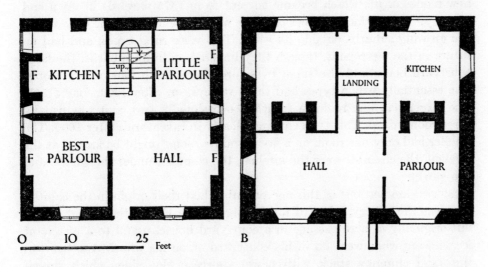

FIGURE 8. Two examples of a novel design of the seventeenth century: the 'double pile', two rooms deep. This plan had usually been avoided hitherto, because of the difficulty of making an efficient roof. The house on the left was built by a Lincolnshire gentleman farmer at Brant Broughton in 1658. It is roofed in two spans, with a valley between. The other, High House, Penrhos, Monmouthshire, is dated 1675, and has a rather eccentric appearance, for it is roofed in a single span which gives a pyramid effect. (The plan on the left is reproduced from *The English Farmhouse and Cottage* (Routledge and Kegan Paul), that on the right from *Monmouthshire Houses*, volume iii (National Museum of Wales).)

or leather for boots, but not timber for wagons or iron for plough parts. The poorer the domestic craftsman, the more likely he was to use a downstairs room as his workshop. Most craftsmen were part-time farmers as well, but in regions such as the West Riding, where the textile industry was now concentrated and weavers worked for more than a local market, the looms were busier and the stock and gear required more space. Then the weaver either had to have a special building, or else move his looms upstairs into a chamber. This process began in West Yorkshire about 1700.

In spite of this great improvement in standards of comfort and convenience in the homes of most classes, there was surprisingly little change in ideas of sanitation. By the seventeenth century no garderobes were built in the new houses of the rich, for this was the age of the close stool: that is, a chair with its seat pierced to hold a pot. Not one farmhouse in a hundred possessed such a luxury: only the chamber pot, of earthenware or pewter for night use, and for the day that 'foul privy' which Tusser recommended should be emptied at night and its contents buried in the garden, to make 'very many things better to grow'.

Although scarcely a domestic building remains of Tudor and early Stuart London, documents show how much the capital contributed to the new modes of life which became current from 1575 onwards in town and country.[9] Four principal types of house were to be found in the City and in the growing suburbs outside its walls. Two were rural types, and had no future in the metropolis, though they lingered on in its suburbs: the large courtyard house and the small two-storey house with four or five rooms. The essentially urban types had three storeys, or, after 1600, four ⟨110⟩. The larger had one room in front, or occasionally two, and was usually three rooms deep. This type emerges clearly in inventories after 1600. The smaller had only one room on a floor, and its rooms might be known as the kitchen, the chamber over the kitchen, the chamber under the garret, and the garret.

Several innovations of this age probably had their origin in the capital. One was the gallery, adopted for prestige in the Elizabethan great house, but originally a mere passage in a courtyard house, useful to a merchant for viewing what went on in his courtyard or on his wharf. Another was the axial chimney stack with newel staircase alongside, which spread throughout the midlands and into Wales by the eighteenth century. Nearly every London house had a kitchen throughout the period, and by 1625, when dining rooms were common, the hall often disappeared. Countrymen who began, after about 1600, to call their hall a kitchen, where it was still used for cooking, probably took the habit from London cousins. Large houses commonly had a wash-house, and that amenity was soon copied, first in Kent. Many small craftsmen had to work in cellar or garret; a silk weaver named Rabio Holland had seven looms and eight spinning wheels in his garret in 1634, two generations earlier than any proven Yorkshire example of the 'top shop'.

London was equally the source from which minor improvements were diffused. Glazed windows seem to have become popular from about 1450 onwards, a century earlier than in the countryside. Similarly, window curtains were to be found by 1660 in every room of even small houses—a necessary amenity in a crowded city. The close stool and pan were to be found in very many houses from about 1575. A good many houses had lead cisterns for water storage. Londoners were distinctly ahead of the provinces in adopting the habit of putting rush matting on the floor, especially in chambers; carpets placed on the floor, instead of on tables or cupboards, began to appear in a few wealthy houses in the seventeenth century.

Londoners then could only continue to keep pace with the growth of their city by crowding their houses together, and by building upwards. Even so, there was more than one way of disposing of families in tall buildings. The London way was to keep the house self-contained, shut off by walls from neighbouring houses—so much so that a Frenchman, visiting London later, wrote that the Londoner's agility in running up and down three or four flights of stairs reminded him of 'a cage with its sticks and birds'. Edinburgh and Glasgow also had to build upwards, from the early seventeenth century onwards, to accommodate a growing population ⟨109⟩. To an English visitor, the soaring tenements of Edinburgh are a most remarkable sight, both for their height—some had in the seventeenth century twice as many floors as the tallest houses built in London after the Fire—and for the vernacular flavour of their architecture: external stair turrets, tall and narrow window openings, roof lines with stepped gables and crowded with chimneys. And yet within there is a complete contrast both with the Scottish tower houses and with London's new houses, for the divisions between families are still, as they have been since the seventeenth century, horizontal and not vertical. Thus, although the tower house made this immensely important contribution to the architectural traditions of modern Scottish housing, the middle and lower classes adapted it to their deeply rooted preference for living on one floor. In such a tenement one floor comprised a house; the staircase was open to the world and the householder needed his doorkey only when he had climbed to his own floor. The best houses were those on the lower floors, and any tenement might shelter families of very varied means. Even so, standards for all were simpler than in England, and two rooms were the average, even for merchants.

Within the house even those simple standards called for one important innovation. All but the poorest English in the sixteenth and seventeenth centuries came to regard a separate room for sleeping as essential. Not so the Scots, but they could make a two-roomed dwelling more tidy, and more secluded after retiring, by boxing in the beds in each room ⟨229⟩. The habit of having beds in a living room is of widespread antiquity; as standards improved in the seventeenth century and onwards the beds were concealed and made to look like wainscotting, or cupboards of an undefined sort.

The best evidence for new building in English towns of the seventeenth century comes from east-coast ports, for they were thriving then as the North Sea herring fishery had reached its peak (fig 3). By the nineteenth century trade with the New World swung the balance of activity to the west-coast ports, and places like King's Lynn, Yarmouth and Folkestone became backwaters in which much seventeenth-century housing has survived. The narrow spit of sand on which Yarmouth had developed was laid out in typically long, narrow properties, and the passages through them had become public thoroughfares, along each side of which small fishermen's cottages faced one another ⟨The Town, 59⟩. In the boom which followed the making of a new haven the houses were rebuilt not in timber, since that was now forbidden, but in brick and flint, or, after about 1640, in brick alone. Naturally the new designs had the usual vertical emphasis of town houses and their one medieval feature—a through passage to the yard at the back—disappeared after 1640. The smaller dwellings had three rooms, one above the other. The ground floor was the 'low room' and had its fireplace on the side wall, flanked by a cupboard and by a newel stair leading to the chamber above and then to the garret, which was used for storing fishing nets and the like. Some houses already had a lean-to kitchen, buttery or wash-house in the yard. Mariners with a share in the trade with Dutch ports, taking stockings and other textiles and bringing back a great variety of continental manufactures, made a comfortable living. Edmund Wilson, mariner, who died in 1674, lived in a house with two rooms on a floor and two and a half storeys. Like many East Anglian folk, he called his living room the kitchen, not the hall, since it was used for cooking. Apart from pots (mostly brass) and fire-irons, the pewter amounted to 50 or 60 lb., and such items as a deal dresser, a looking-glass and a warming-pan were now making their appearance in houses of this class. The parlour was furnished as a sitting room—a long table for meals, six red-leather chairs, four buffet stools and a 'dornock' carpet (made in Doornijk, better known now as Tournay) to go on the table between meals; a case to hold drinking glasses and two pictures on the walls, two bibles and other books. There were also two bedsteads, perhaps kept for visitors. The kitchen chamber was used only for lumber, and the parlour chamber was the principal sleeping room: it had chairs, stools, trunks for clothing, a small table with a blue carpet, pictures and looking-glasses on the walls, and two bedsteads—one posted, with curtains and valances, the other a truckle bed. The garret, or 'vance roof' as East Anglians called it, had another bed, all the household linen and typical stores: peas, spun yarn, a coil of new ropes, sea-chests and fire-arms.

The Rural House since 1660

THE GREAT HOUSES built after 1688 represent the ultimate triumph of the architect over the domestic traditions of the Middle Ages. The magnates had always needed to impress, either with a show of armed or liveried followers, or by the way they could entertain royalty. In the great houses of Elizabeth's reign, scale, and such symbols of status as enormous windows and ranks of chimneys, mattered most. Masons such as Smythson had only modified the customary internal design of the house. In the early Stuart period the houses designed by Inigo Jones or influenced by his ideas (Raynham Park, Coleshill etc.) were designed to impress more subtly, by their scholarly use of Renaissance ideas both in external design and in interior ornament. More significant, the freedom of a new design provided a chance to reconsider the function and relation of rooms; in the process medieval ideas vanished entirely. The medieval great hall had been a public room, in which those of lower rank found themselves placed below the salt, but not excluded. In the great house of Jones's design, which became the common ideal after 1660, the hall was no more than an entrance lobby ⟨136⟩, an anteroom to the saloon ⟨137⟩ and the suite of rooms connected with it. There the aristocracy entertained its equals.

The new houses of the aristocracy thus reflect the widening gulf between rich and poor which characterised society from the sixteenth to the nineteenth centuries. Pratt's Coleshill (1650) had a frontage of 120 ft.; Castle Howard, built fifty years later by Vanbrugh for the immensely wealthy Earl of Carlisle, is over 600 ft. in length ⟨135⟩, and Marlborough's Blenheim 850 ft. The richest landowning families of the century and a half after 1714 enjoyed incomes far larger than the most powerful medieval barons, and their rural palaces represented a dominance more civilised but no less real. A compact design was out of keeping with the grandeur of scale and splendour of finish now desired. Pope wrote in 1731:

47

> 'At Timon's villa let us pass a day,
> Where all cry out, "What sums are thrown away!"
> So proud, so grand, of that stupendous air,
> Soft and agreeable were never there.'

Kyp's *Britannia Illustrata* (1708) and Campbell's *Vitruvius Britannicus* (1717), with their drawings of country houses, found a very ready market; sight-seeing became fashionable, and one Georgian duke charged his visitors a fee.[10]

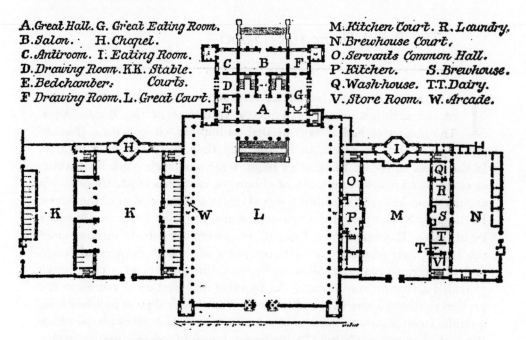

A. *Great Hall.* G. *Great Eating Room.*
B. *Salon.* H. *Chapel.*
C. *Antiroom.* I. *Eating Room.*
D. *Drawing Room.* KK. *Stable.*
E. *Bedchamber.* *Courts.*
F. *Drawing Room.* L. *Great Court.*

M. *Kitchen Court.* R. *Laundry.*
N. *Brewhouse Court.*
O. *Servants Common Hall.*
P. *Kitchen.* S. *Brewhouse.*
Q. *Wash-house.* T.T. *Dairy.*
V. *Store Room.* W. *Arcade.*

FIGURE 9. Plan of Eastbury Park, Dorset, designed by Vanbrugh for George Dodding-ton and his nephew Bubb Doddington. It was completed in 1738, and was exceeded in size only by Blenheim and Castle Howard. This plan, taken from Campbell's *Vitruvius Britannicus*, shows the main block (A–G) flanked by wings each surrounding double courtyards. Only part of the stable wing now survives. (Reproduced from *Country Houses of Dorset*, Country Life.)

Within less than a century the vogue for such immense houses faded, but it had produced some of Britain's finest buildings. They can scarcely be judged as houses. They all had only one principal floor, the first, following the designs of Palladio, the Renaissance architect. Hence, extension of the plan was inevitable (see figure 9). It took the form of adding two or four wings to the central block, connected either by a mere corridor or by a string of rooms; in a few instances the wings were meant to appear detached, and were connected only by underground passages. How the three or five units were designed, in terms of use, varied a good deal. If the kitchens were kept in the central block the wings could be used for a chapel, a library or for guest rooms. More commonly they were used for kitchens, stables, laundry, brewhouse and the like. Only in one of the latest of these extraordinary houses—Ickworth, built in the last years of the eighteenth century by Frederick Hervey, Bishop of Derry and 4th Earl of Bristol—was the logic of this sort of design accepted: one of the two wings was built first and designed as the residence, while the central block, a tall rotunda never completed in the bishop's lifetime, was afterwards finished for use only when entertaining.

In the design of the central block of the Palladian great house the impression made on the guest was the paramount consideration. Hence the emphasis on the entrance hall and staircase, which were sometimes combined. In addition to the saloon—a large reception room, entered from the hall—there was always a drawing room ⟨138⟩, or more than one, and sometimes a dining room for state occasions. Houghton had a 'Marble Parlour' for state dinners; the family when alone ate in 'the Parlour or common dining room'.[11] The remainder of the principal floor was taken up with bedrooms (or 'dressing rooms' as they are often labelled on plans) for distinguished guests. Very few of these great houses had a chapel; indeed, one might say that its place in household life at this social level was taken by the library, which in later Georgian mansions was often a fine room ⟨140⟩.

Apart from the relatively few 'prodigy houses'—Summerson's term for the great Elizabethan houses seems even more appropriate for the grandest monuments of Baroque and Palladian design—scores of more modest country houses were built between 1690 and 1760, usually designed by mason-contractors rather than by gentlemen-architects, whether amateur or professional ⟨144⟩. Their houses perpetuated the late seventeenth-century plan, and took their architectural features from some admired example. As the eighteenth century wore on, the demand for country houses of reasonable dimensions outweighed the demand for palaces, for there was a limit to the number of incomes that could survive the cost of a Castle Howard or a Houghton. The number and wealth of the landed gentry was still growing and those who had made a fortune in trade or industry swelled the class. For such men the Palladian architect had created precisely the type of house required—the *villa*. The earliest villas, such as Colin Campbell's Mereworth, were the playthings of great men; as houses they involved such devices as carrying chimney flues up in the skin of a central dome. But the villa became by the middle of the eighteenth century something entirely suitable, from its scale, for a modest and restful retirement—'more in the nature of a retreat than an advertisement of its owner's standing or ability to entertain'.[12] From beginnings in the home counties the type was dispersed throughout the countryside, by the assiduous authors of pattern books for architects ⟨181, 182⟩, and also by the architects themselves, a fully professionalised class by the end of the century.

Under the patronage of the Georgian gentry and the upper middle class, the villa type became standardised as a house with two rooms in front flanking an entrance hall, and two or three rooms deep. Two staircases were placed in the centre of a more or less square plan, and there was no saloon. The principal rooms were now on the ground floor again— Robert Adam was the first architect to bring the architectural order, if it was used, down to ground level. Kitchens and other service rooms had then to be provided in a wing built on a smaller scale and concealed by shrubs behind the main block. The villa thus merges into the type of symmetrically fronted farmhouse, with five windows on its front, which had become common from the early eighteenth century onwards ⟨126⟩; but given a pillared porch, if not an ordered portico, it could rank as a villa. The farmer rarely adopted such a pretentious design, even for the many entirely new farmhouses built in midland England on the farms created by the enclosure of open fields. Country parsons, on the other hand, were anxious to show by the style of their parsonages that they belonged to the gentry, as indeed many of them did by birth. Many a parsonage was either rebuilt during the course of the century, or enlarged, and the new building had almost invariably architectural qualities absent in farmhouses—a pillared porch; a façade with a pediment, however mean; a drawing room with a bowed end, or sashed windows down to the ground ⟨133⟩. Such houses belonged to successful pluralists, for very few country livings could singly support such a style. Nearly half the country parsonages at the end of the eighteenth century still had only two or three rooms on a floor, and they very rarely had a parson resident in them. They were sufficient for a curate, or else were let to farm labourers.

The successful farmer, although he was not seduced by architectural pattern books, was ready to listen to his wife's ideas of how the interior of his house should be finished. The best parlour, which already had a boarded floor, must be wainscotted chair high, and papered above ⟨146⟩. The best chamber was also hung with paper, but the remaining rooms had only whitewashed walls. The old, dusty earth floors could be replaced by brick, and the hall flagged with stone. Ceilings downstairs could be underdrawn with plaster, concealing the joists and keeping in warmth; bedrooms ceiled so that they were no longer open to the thatch.

In northern England and Wales the influence of pattern books was much less widespread. Architect-designed houses were thinner on the ground;

the plan of the farmhouse was more likely to display its local ancestry. The most striking local plan in the north is the square house more or less identical in plan with the southern double pile (see figure 8), but roofed with one wide and rather flat pitch. It had four rooms on the ground floor —living kitchen, parlour, with back kitchen and dairy behind—and four bedrooms upstairs. It was the most popular plan for new houses in the Lake District from 1750 to 1850, and it was imported into Wales early in the nineteenth century. Cottages were still built with only one storey ⟨116⟩; indeed a ballad describing how Lake District communities combined to help a young man build his mud-walled cottage was still current in the early nineteenth century.

These contrasts of highland and lowland zone on the eve of the Industrial Revolution reflect two different societies. In Norfolk the prosperous farmer and his wife no longer sat with the farm workers of an evening. In the Lake District they were still, and continued to be until the present century, members of the family rather than employees; the only distinction in the home was that the farmer and his family took their meals at a small round table drawn up to the fire, while the servants ate at the long table under the window ⟨119⟩. The lowland farmer could only get and keep his large labour force by building, or buying, cottages—'tied' cottages—as Norfolk landlords had done for a century and more. In the north cottages were very scarce; farmers erected none, and those built by farm workers for themselves were naturally cheaply constructed and simply planned. Of their plan nothing can be said since all have vanished, but they may still have had room for the cottager's cow under the same roof.

In Wales, prior to enclosure and consolidation of farms in the nineteenth century, rural society included very many small crofters whose dwellings could be reckoned as cottages, since they had no farm buildings round them ⟨91⟩. Almost all had a fireplace at the gable end, an arrangement typical of the cottages of the highland zone ⟨92, 93⟩. Some single-roomed cottages persisted to within living memory. That simple structure could be made into two rooms by placing the dresser so that it divided living and sleeping parts. Otherwise a partition could be made of cloth, or of lath and reeds, sometimes no more than head height. Another way to make life more seemly was to box in the beds at the further end of the house— a 'cupboard bed' in the Welsh tradition. Many of these cottages were given a half-loft (*croglofft*) over the chamber (*siambr*) or sleeping half of the house ⟨200⟩, beside which was a tiny dairy. If beds filled all the further end, a dairy could be contrived at the gable end, alongside the hearth, for dairy there had to be. In such *croglofft* cottages the entrance was usually in the centre of one side, and the comfort of the hearth then required a speer or screen, making a short passage inside the doorway. Near the slate

51

quarries that screen was made of a single slab of slate. Only in the parts of Wales most open to English influence did the two-storey cottage make its appearance.

The transformation of rural housing which had begun in Elizabethan England began to affect Scotland from the end of the seventeenth century and the process has only recently been completed. Improvements consisted of the use of more durable building materials, enlargement of the accommodation, or even the adoption of an entirely novel plan and design. It is easy to put these forms into a typological order but impossible, in the present state of our knowledge, to give individual examples, or even particular types, a firm date. The simplest of all was the turf house, or sod house, which has been recorded in many parts of the Scottish Highlands, as well as in the Isle of Man ⟨199⟩. A more efficient and in general more recent form had earth walls faced inside and out with stone, and also stone gables. Such houses were naturally of one storey. Stone walled houses with very crudely made cruck trusses for the roof were still being built in the eighteenth century. Where neither good timber nor workable stone was available, as in the Isle of Mull, houses were simple in the extreme, with entrances only three feet high, lacking any door, and everywhere in the Highlands a central open hearth, under a hole in the roof, must have been the usual thing.

The common type of house was certainly the long house, with a cow-house separated by a through passage or 'through gang' from the living end. The only distinction between the crofter and the small proprietor or laird was that the latter might have three or four rooms, each leading to the next, instead of the minimal two. Much more usually there were two rooms only in the living end—the kitchen and the 'spence'. In the first the household cooking was done and meals taken; there the family worked and chatted, sitting round an open hearth or under a great chimney hood at the gable end ⟨227, 228⟩; there they slept, in their box beds. The inner room must have been originally a storeroom alone, from its name—a spence is a buttery—but was now on the way to becoming a parlour as well; it contained the best furniture as well as stores, and was used when important guests called. Occasionally the roof space was lofted over, to be used for articles not in everyday use, or even as a bedchamber. In a prosperous Renfrew farmhouse of 1826 the furniture of the living kitchen consisted of a long table for household meals and a small table or buffet stool for occasional refreshments, a dresser and shelves for pewter and earthenware, a form or two and a few hardwood chairs, the ubiquitous chests for linen: little different from a farmhouse kitchen anywhere in the island in 1775. Equally common were the mirror or seeing glass on the wall, and the grandfather clock which regulated the working day as inescapably as did the factory buzzer in a nineteenth-century town. The terms 'but' and 'ben' came into general usage for such houses, but varied in connotation. They meant simply *without* and *within*, so that in the smallest crofter's cottage 'but' meant the animals' end, 'ben' the living end, but in larger houses to 'go ben' meant to go from the living kitchen to the inner room. Confusion in the use of the terms suggests a twofold origin: a house might be enlarged either by turning the animals out of the byre or by adding a room at the other end of the building.

Into this native way of life a new and imported element found its way —the storeyed symmetrical house ⟨130⟩. It was reduced for Scottish use to its simplest form—two storeys only, two rooms on the ground floor on either side of a central entrance, with staircase opposite the entrance and

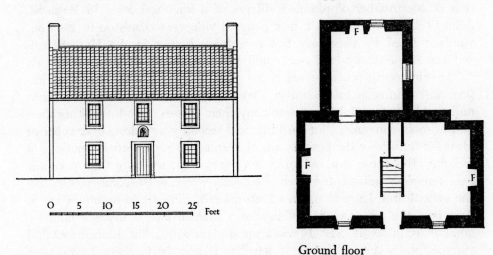

Ground floor

FIGURE 10. House at Airth, Stirlingshire, dated 1730. This type, with symmetrical façade, two storeys throughout, staircase in the centre and fireplaces at the gable ends, was being built throughout the island in the eighteenth century, though it naturally had higher social status in Scotland than in the south. In this case there seems to have been no attempt to make use of the roof space, and the ground-floor rooms may well have had box beds originally. The back room may have been added later.

fireplaces at the gable ends (see figure 10). It appeared first about 1700 in the ports of the eastern seaboard, as suitable for ships' captains, merchants and excise officials, but during the next hundred and fifty years it was widely adopted in the countryside by small lairds and by the new class of 'farmers' created by agricultural improvements ⟨197⟩. Accommodation was very simple and the pattern of life in such houses was influenced by the first-floor hall tradition of the Scottish tower house, rather than by the English tradition of day rooms downstairs and night rooms above.

Scottish villages, as distinct from the isolated Highland croft, had their own housing revolution in the late eighteenth and early nineteenth centuries. The impetus came from improving landlords. The general standard which was now abandoned is shown by the remains of the crofters' settlements in Sutherland and elsewhere which were cleared by powerful landlords early in the nineteenth century. Houses were usually either about 30 ft. in length or about 60 ft.; each group stood within a stone wall, with some detached farm building, one corn-drying kiln for the community, and kail yards (or vegetable gardens to a Sassenach) to some of the houses.

The improving movement spread northwards from the Lothians, and depended on capital to build new houses and start industries such as knitting, weaving and spinning. An effort to improve fisheries began in 1786, and most of the distilleries date from after 1824. The result was a remarkable number of planned villages of a kind unknown in England. John Cockburn, who built a new planned village at Ormiston in 1735 onwards, refused to allow any but two-storey houses in the High Street, but the single-storey tradition could not be entirely dislodged ⟨222–4⟩.

The nineteenth-century farmhouse thus represents the results of improvements in economic conditions which began in the sixteenth century, and enabled successful farmers to copy their betters, first by making their houses more convenient for working, and secondly by taking over superior ideas for furnishing the best rooms, or even adopting architects' notions of building. But these new notions were, very often, no more than a veneer over tenacious habits, and even if superior ways had become acceptable, the agricultural depression after 1880 made it difficult to maintain them. As a boy, the writer spent holidays in a Lincolnshire farmhouse built by an ancestor in about 1840. It was a square box with a flat, hipped roof and stuccoed walls; a smaller box attached to it was the kitchen. Two copper beeches planted in 1840 flanked the path to the front door, but it was never used. Every foot followed as a matter of course the flagged path to the kitchen door. Neither of the two parlours was ever used. The servants' loft over the kitchen, reached by a ladder from the kitchen, was empty. The kitchen was the living room; meals were cooked and eaten there, bread was baked; the box mangle was no longer used, but its big top made a convenient second table; there was not a single piece of upholstered furniture. From the kitchen one went to the dairy at the back of the house, or past the closed doors of the parlours and past the grandfather clock on the landing to bedrooms where, for a child, getting into a feather bed was like climbing on to a hill top. Other farmhouses have left different but complementary impressions. One, formerly a manor house, seemed haunted by the maidservants who once slept in attics lighted only by a tiny skylight, scrubbed acres of brick floor, swept endless passages and carried coals for innumerable fires—in the scullery a cooking range, a washing copper and

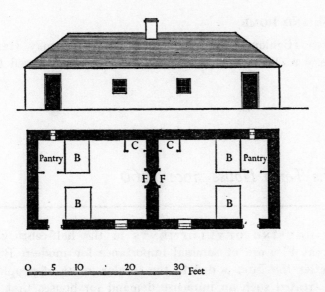

FIGURE 11. Design for model agricultural labourers' cottages in Scotland, reproduced from Sir John Sinclair's *General Report of the Agriculture and Political Circumstances of Scotland* (1812), one of the many reports of this time which deal not only with farming techniques and problems, but also with rural housing. In contrast to the English cottages shown in figure 14, Scottish cottages were at this time of one storey only, with fewer, but larger, rooms. Note the box beds (B), cupboards (C) and fireplaces (F).

a brewing copper; in the kitchen another range and a coal-fired hot plate; fires in study, dining room and drawing room. Still a third house, in the south, had pathetic pretensions. The long conservatory by the side of the house had a vine; full-length mirrors at opposite ends of the drawing room reflected the light like an underground train on a curve, since the walls of the old house were not regular and the mirror faces not quite parallel; the water closet upstairs, flushed by rainwater collected from the roof, worked perfectly in wet weather.

Since 1940 the revolution in government policy toward agriculture has transformed the life of farming families. A farm on very poor Nottinghamshire soil, christened derisively 'Labour in Vain' when it was built in the enclosure period, had, in 1950, a Jaguar car standing in the yard, a washing machine in the scullery, a radio and a television set in the living kitchen. New windows and ceilings, Marley-tiled floors, Aga cookers, parlours becoming genuine living rooms thanks to the vacuum cleaner and the television set—an old way of life and its material embodiments are vanishing more rapidly than ever before. Only the basic contrast of highland and lowland zone is still beyond the power of the scientific farmer to eradicate. The remote farms of the highland zone still take what they will from lowland culture but keep what seems essential of their own. Electricity

55

may light a Highland croft, and a television set may stand by the hearth fire in a Devonshire farmhouse, but less has changed than might appear.

The Town House since 1660

LONDON HOUSING DEVELOPMENTS in the half-century following the Great Fire are of seminal importance for modern Britain. The crisis after the Fire, added to the regular influx of people from the provinces, created such an immense demand for houses that large-scale capitalist enterprise got its first opportunity in this field. The entrepreneurs were aristocrats such as the Earl of Southampton and the Earl of St. Albans, who saw more profit in this sort of activity than in coal-mining or other industries, and speculators of lesser social standing but greater acuity like Nicholas Barbon. The conditions naturally led to uniform and economic planning, controls which were reinforced by the standards of architectural design adopted in Charles I's time, under the influence of Inigo Jones, and also by the fire regulations enforced by the City after 1666. In the eighteenth century another unifying factor was added: the pattern books produced by the score from which builders could take their designs ⟨181, 182⟩. For the first time the English middle-class family accepted the idea of living in a house identical—precisely so, or else a mirror image—with that of next-door neighbours. The 'terrace house' was born. New houses such as those in Red Lion Square, developed by Barbon in 1684 onwards, or elsewhere in the West End by great Whig and Tory landowners in the eighteenth century, were the ancestors not only of Georgian Bath ⟨The Town, 95⟩, or a fashionable Victorian suburb like Clifton in Bristol ⟨185⟩, but also of the back streets of our industrial towns ⟨207⟩. The scale may vary, and the architectural historian's verdict may range from admiration verging on reverence to contempt for the designer and pity for the occupants, but the internal design is broadly the same.

The essence of the design was two rooms on a floor, with a staircase. Beyond that, infinite variations could be played on the simple theme (figure 12). The staircase was difficult to light. In better-class houses it had a roof light ⟨162⟩; in small Victorian houses it was quite dark unless doors were left open. It could be placed at the side of the house or, if frontages were narrow, between front and back rooms and parallel with the street. The greatest variation was in the width of the frontage. Georgian houses built for middle-class families might be only 24 ft. wide (see figure 12), working-class houses of 1870 half that or even less. The former had an entrance hall that was at least a wide passage; in the latter the passage had to be sacrificed and entrance was directly into the 'front room' (figure 13).

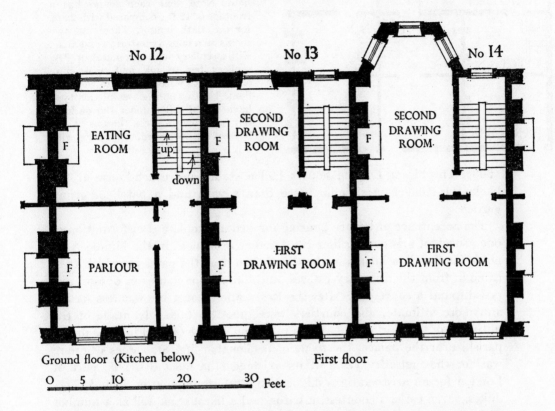

Ground floor (Kitchen below)   First floor

0   5 .10   20   30 Feet

FIGURE 12. Plan of terrace houses in Alfred Street, Bath, built in 1772. There are two rooms to a floor with kitchen and scullery in the basement (not shown), family rooms on the ground floor, drawing rooms *en suite* on the first floor and bedrooms and garrets above. While the fronts are uniform, bay windows and other modifications, either original or added, were permissible at the back.

The basement common to the whole range might have rooms of the same size as those on higher floors, reasonably well lit in front and perfectly lit at the back, or else be only a dark hole with no more light than came through a grating on the pavement, down which coal supplies were delivered ⟨165, 207⟩. From the earliest phase a room might be added at the rear of less than the full width of the plot—a closet in the seventeenth-century houses, or kitchen, scullery, wash-house, privy in later times

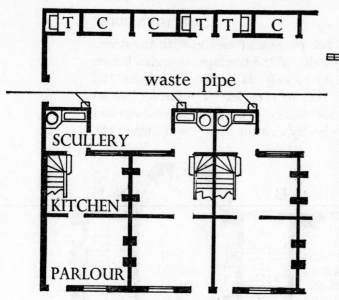

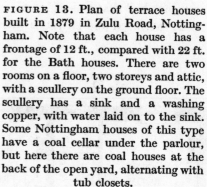

FIGURE 13. Plan of terrace houses built in 1879 in Zulu Road, Nottingham. Note that each house has a frontage of 12 ft., compared with 22 ft. for the Bath houses. There are two rooms on a floor, two storeys and attic, with a scullery on the ground floor. The scullery has a sink and a washing copper, with water laid on to the sink. Some Nottingham houses of this type have a coal cellar under the parlour, but here there are coal houses at the back of the open yard, alternating with tub closets.

⟨208⟩. The bigger London houses had a stable and coach-house at the back; the smaller version no more than a yard and a patch of grimy garden.

The acceptance of terrace housing implied a complete transformation of one aspect of aristocratic life: the London residence. In the Middle Ages noble families had houses in the City, often near the gates by which they came in from their country estates, and like manor houses in design, disposed round a courtyard. After the Restoration, court life was less formal and more intimate, and courtiers were quick to take advantage of the initiative of the Earl of St. Albans in taking a lease of land in St. James's parish, near the palace, the focus of fashionable life. St. James's Square was for the first fifty years of its existence the most desirable part of London for an aristocratic residence. In 1721 its population included six dukes, seven earls, a countess, a baron and a baronet as well as a number of foreign ambassadors. The houses were not entirely typical of London development of this age; they had larger frontages, and though their exteriors were restrained and modest enough in design, as contemporary taste dictated, they had quite splendid facilities for entertainment. Money was lavished on stucco work and imported marble; frescoes and architectural paintings done by foreign artists supplanted the native tradition of wainscot and tapestry. The arrangement of the rooms shows the real purpose of the houses. The kitchen and other services were as usual in the basement, with stables round the court at the rear. The front door opened on to a porter's hall with the entrance hall proper beyond it, from which a grand staircase led to the first floor where guests were received. The 'eating room' or parlour was on the ground floor; sometimes there was a

58

library, or the dressing room of the master of the house and a powdering room, with a water closet adjacent to it. There was of course always a second staircase for servants. For entertaining, the first floor had two or even three drawing rooms; sometimes the largest served as a music room. The lady of the house might have her dressing room (with powdering room and water closet) at the rear of this floor. The top floor had bedrooms for family or for guests; servants slept in the garret or over the coach-house and stables at the rear. The square remained largely residential until a century ago, and all the great Georgian architects had a hand in rebuilding or altering houses in it according to the current aristocratic taste and means.

The idea of having the principal reception room on the first floor in middle- and upper-class houses is a most direct product of the Renaissance, adopted by the early eighteenth-century designers who took as their model the Italian Palladio, and accepted as fashionable by those who had made the Grand Tour and stayed on the *piano nobile* (best floor) of Italian hotels and villas. It also reinforced any latent relics of the ancient tradition of the first-floor hall house; certainly in Scotland the idea fell in entirely with native tradition, and in Edinburgh the first-floor drawing room became and remained a normal feature of middle-class self-contained houses. Principally, however, it accorded with the confined conditions of town life. With kitchen and storerooms in the basement, meals could most conveniently be served on the ground floor, and reception rooms for large parties could then only be placed on the floor above. In London, however, the most characteristic feature is that the ground floor is no more than two or three steps above street level. This was brought about not so much by excavating for the basement as by raising the street level; while the front basement room looks out into the deep 'area' between the frontage of the house and its railings, the back leads straight out into a court little below the natural level.[13] This design appears in the great development of post-Restoration London for which speculators like Nicholas Barbon were responsible, and no doubt grew out of a medieval tradition of cellars half below ground, but the neat arrangement of raised roadway retained by the area wall was an ingenious novelty of this age. The crowning stroke was to use the space under the pavement for a coal store ⟨160⟩.

The design of the London terrace house was naturally adopted for the middle- and upper-class houses built by the hundred in eighteenth-century Bath, and for rows of houses in smaller towns like Stamford or Exeter, where successful merchants and attorneys were a thriving element in the community and where the lesser gentry had town houses. Basement kitchen, grand staircase to first-floor drawing room, very tall sashed windows—all the London elements are there. The grand effect of several drawing rooms *en suite* with lofty double doors between could be imitated

59

by having only a folding screen between dining room and drawing room, a device particularly popular in the west of England ⟨164⟩. Edinburgh was for a time shaken out of the native tradition by the impact of this fashion for terraces of self-contained houses, but only for a time. When the development of the New Town began in 1760, north of the steep-sided valley in which the railway now runs, the first terraces were divided vertically into self-contained houses, but eventually the same exterior design was adapted to tenements or maisonettes. Elsewhere, the tenement tradition was undisturbed, and eventually tall blocks, usually of four floors with a house on each floor, sprang up in what seem the most unlikely places ⟨172⟩. From about 1800 onwards, some Edinburgh tenements no longer had a staircase open to every caller, however undesirable. The one entrance had a locked door which the householder could open without going downstairs, by an arrangement of chains and pulleys, provided that a view of the top of the caller's head from an open window was satisfactory. Though these tenements may look like fortresses on the outskirts of Edinburgh and in industrial Dundee, and though they may degenerate into undesirable slums in the Gorbals, they give the centre of a town, however small, an essentially *urban* quality which an English town often lacks, and they have helped to prevent class differences becoming as great as in England. Englishmen have escaped tasks which Scots take for granted, such as arranging joint responsibility for sweeping stairs and repairing chimney stacks, or taking a small dustbin downstairs each day, because a large one emptied weekly would become too heavy.

In England the compact and shapely urbanity of terraces, crescents and squares was disrupted in the nineteenth century. 'The villa came to town.'[14] The downward percolation of modes of behaviour which is the most pronounced feature of modern society steadily reduced the villa in scale, and brought it from the depths of the country first to the suburb, within carriage distance of shop, warehouse or office, and then into the town itself. Victorian builders, to make the most profitable use of the land they were swallowing up, adopted one device from the Georgian terrace house, the basement kitchen ⟨184⟩. Another seems to have emerged first in improved housing for farm workers: houses built in pairs, semi-detached ⟨183⟩. The house with hall and parlour and an axial stack between was certainly the ancestor of the new type, for the earliest detached houses were non-parlour cottages. Whole districts of some cities, such as Clifton in Bristol, or north Oxford, are solid colonies of such middle-class houses, and between the wars they came, though without the basement kitchen, within reach of the working classes. The villa, whether semi-detached, two storeys or bungalow, was for a century and a half the Englishman's idea of his own home.

'Ewbank'd inside and Atco'd out, the leaves of the Virginia creeper beside the windows of the best bedroom hardly stir, and even birds only hop—and flutter a few feet in the air, and hop again—along the ornamental ridge of the red-tiled roof.

Inside it is more peaceful still. The sunlight coming through the bottle glass of the front door falls in irregular blotches on the cocoa-nut mat made by blind ex-service men, on the fumed oak hatstand and on the wall-rack holding a variety of walking sticks collected on summer holidays, including one with a spiked ferrule and a sprig of edelweiss cut in the wood below the handle. These blotches of sunlight make the narrow hall seem rather dark by contrast. It smells faintly of furniture polish and somewhat more faintly of the American cloth of which the hood of a folding perambulator is made, a perambulator for which there is really not enough room in the hall, as the visitor will soon discover if he steps too confidently past the foot of the stairs. The far part of the hall is lighter because of the drawing room: a sofa with loose covers in flowered chintz, faded with much laundering, cream paint, the corner of a piano with framed photographs on it and a bay window with leaded panes, the centre part opening to the ground and leading down a couple of steps to the bright garden.'[15]

Words written in 1946 are already out of date—the garage has become essential, the roof is crowned with a television aerial ⟨236⟩—but the Englishman's ideal remains essentially unaltered. In Scotland, however, the villa was, characteristically, turned into Scottish forms. Semi-detached villas in Corstorphine have the same defensive convenience as the tenements: visitors can be observed through a clear pane in the glazed front door, and a handle in the hall wall releases the bolt on the front gate only a few feet away. The flatted villas in other Edinburgh suburbs are even more remarkable to an Englishman than tenements ⟨235⟩. Those built shortly before 1914 may still have a recess in the kitchen for a servant's bed.

The exigencies of modern town life have thrown up one more type of dwelling—terraced building with houses on each side, back to back ⟨214⟩. No historian or architect has made a serious search for the origin of the type. The earliest known examples are a pair in Bermondsey, built in 1706, but they are not artisans' houses, and the type never became common in London.[16] They are indistinguishable in principle from what Seebohm Rowntree called 'not-throughs' when he found them in York in 1900; they consist of terraced cottages with a living room and a scullery down and two bedrooms up; they have only the one entrance, and no door or window on the other side ⟨209⟩. It would be unhistorical to blame the speculative builder for this peculiarity; the design stems from that of earlier cottages, which had only one entrance. Coals had to be carried in through the living room, if there was space to store them inside, but at least the room was snug as could be.

The earliest houses built by the Strutts at Belper and Milford were cottages of this plan, but with doors and small gardens back and front. Those in Hopping Terrace, Milford, have a living room 14 ft. square, with a scullery behind 9 ft. by 8 ft. and a staircase making up the rectangle; there are two bedrooms above. All the details of plan and construction display the thought given by the Strutts to every aspect of the life of the community they were creating. Adjacent houses in Belper have interlocking plans. There and at Milford one can see window frames, adjustable gutter brackets, door numbers and drain-hole covers, all cast in the firm's own foundry. When, however, more houses were needed, and only the steeper slopes of the hillside were available near at hand, some ingenious architect designed East and West Terrace in a back-to-back form. Each house has the same basic accommodation, and the plans again interlock, every other house on each side having a cellar dug into the hillside. Each house is internally 18 ft. by 9 ft. (excluding the cellar), so that a pair takes up only about 20 ft. by 21 ft.

In the narrow West Riding valleys, where road, railway and mill took up the flat of the valley bottom, back-to-backs were inevitable, or some variant: backs-to-earth, or four-storey terraces consisting of two rows one on top of the other, a road at ground-floor level on one side and another at third-floor level on the other ⟨217⟩. In nineteenth-century towns, houses like these, built back to back or round a narrow court with a row of privies in the centre, were run up as speculation by bricklayers, joiners, glaziers or painters, or else owned by small tradesmen and publicans. They rented at about 2s. 6d. per week.

The immense volume of new housing created by the Industrial Revolution in the north was dreary in its lack of any architectural quality, varied in the accommodation it provided, disgraceful in the squalor it imposed on families ⟨210, 211⟩. But underneath the visual qualities given by architect and speculative builder to industrial housing lay solid social traditions, little changed by the demands of industrial life. The English cottage home, if one can use the term in a sociological sense without any undertones of patronage or overtones of the romantic, had evolved in the sixteenth and seventeenth centuries from a single room to a house with living room, an unheated scullery or a larder and one or two bedrooms upstairs. Sleeping and living must be separated, though cooking, eating and living in one room were perfectly acceptable. North of a line from York to Chester, this set of domestic habits came to be adopted in the eighteenth and nineteenth centuries, but north of the Border it simply failed to make headway

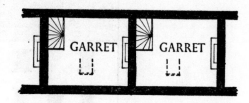

GARRET

Ground floor

First Floor

0 5 10   20   30 Feet

FIGURE 14. Farm labourers' cottages at the time of the Napoleonic war. The row of two-storey cottages with garrets was built at Bletchingdon, Oxfordshire, in 1796. Each has a living kitchen, larder, one bedroom and a garret. The rooms are smaller than in Scottish cottages (figure 11). These Oxfordshire cottages had an earth closet in the garden, and a washhouse added more recently.

(see figure 11). 'The Scottish way of life had been got by ancient country habit out of ancient town necessity, and it was a one- or two-room way, very tough and indestructible.'[17] Many young couples expected, certainly up to 1940 and perhaps since, to be able to start married life in a 'single end', with the idea of getting a 'double end' later, and so single-room dwellings were still being built in this century, and in 1914 nearly half the population lived in houses of one or two rooms. Those two were generally larger than in an English house, though how much larger no statistician can tell us. David Dale in his tenements at New Lanark gave each weaver two rooms, both with box beds (see figure 16). Kennet Village, east of Clackmannan, built before 1800 for coal-miners, consisted of houses with only one storey and an attic, but each had a large garden. Shale-miners' cottages at Broxburn, West Lothian, built in the last third of the nineteenth century, have the same accommodation but no gardens ⟨219⟩

Front elevation

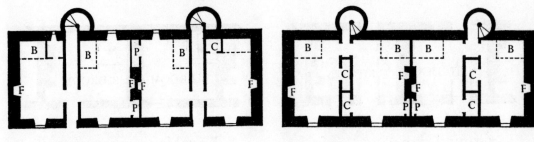

Ground Floor   First Floor

0   10   20   30   40   50 Feet

FIGURE 15. A design for weavers' tenements, prepared for William Wilson, tartan manufacturer, of Bannockburn, 1780. The design provides for eight single-roomed tenements, four on a floor, each with a small closet (C), a press or cupboard (P) and a box bed (B). The block has two external stair turrets, each with a newel stair; compare ⟨172⟩.

The majority of Northumbrian miners' cottages had either two or three rooms; the fact that they did not have box beds probably made sleeping conditions in them less satisfactory. Gardens were rare. The effect of the Industrial Revolution was not to reduce standards of accommodation, but to rob working-class families of the amenities they and their ancestors had enjoyed before they were drawn to the town, and to submit them to the dangers to health created by dense urban building without appropriate sanitary arrangements. The dished slop stone or sink which had been a normal feature of a sixteenth-century manor house was also to be found in the standard Sheffield cottage, though it had there a lead pipe to the sewer or street channel. In Manchester of the 1840s a contemporary described 'the multitude of pigs walking about in all the alleys, rooting in the offal heaps . . .; pork raisers rent the courts and build pig-pens in them'[18]. Rows in Preston in 1860 had at the rear a small yard from which there was no exit; some men kept a pig there, and in the corner was a privy emptying

64

into an open sewer between the rows ⟨210, 211⟩. The contents of the cess-pool at the end belonged to the landlord who no doubt found that the older they were, the higher the price they would fetch. Worst of all, shortage of housing compelled the unfortunate and the feckless to put up with living in cellars never intended for anything but coal; and the blue books show that the inhabited cellars of London or Liverpool were much the most dreadful slums.

In the 1840s and onwards, distillers in Edinburgh built a number of 'colonies' for their own workers which were clearly intended as model dwellings. North of Glenogle Road are several rows of two-storey terraced flats ⟨220⟩. They have basically the same design as back-to-back housing, except that each house runs through the block, and ground floor and first floor are entered from opposite sides. The upper floors have a generous outside stair which gives the row a great deal of character. Many smaller Scottish towns have somewhat similar houses, with a forestair on the street to the first floor, or else one at the rear. It is difficult to tell whether they are an original feature or the result of later subdivision of a two-storey house. All one can say is that the tradition of a stair outside the block, either completely open or in a turret, persisted from the days of tower houses into the Victorian heyday. Newcastle-upon-Tyne invented its own particular version of working-class flats, indistinguishable from terrace housing elsewhere in England except for the paired doors, one of them leading to the upstairs flat ⟨218⟩.

Charitable societies for improving the housing of the poor began to appear in the eighteenth century, but their work only came to substantial fruition in the middle of the nineteenth. Official concern was concentrated first on the problem of housing single men and women—the immigrant Irish labourers whose needs and personal standards everywhere created the worst slums, and single women who were a moral problem. Hence the first housing legislation dealt with common lodging houses (Common Lodging House Act, 1852–53), and much benevolent effort went into provision of that sort. The first working-class housing put up other than by speculators or by industrialists were the Albert Family Dwellings (to distinguish them from lodging houses) in Deal Street, Stepney (1849); they were the work of the Metropolitan Association for Improving the Dwellings of the Poor. They consisted of flats in five-storey blocks and provided homes of four rooms—living kitchen, scullery and two bedrooms; access was gained by 'streets in the air' ⟨212⟩. The scullery had main water and a sink, a dust shoot and a lavatory. There was an elaborate system of ventilation for the drains, to guard against the supposed danger of cholera from the gases in them. Rents in such tall buildings were inevitably high, and the Association also built Albert and Victoria Cottages, of two storeys only, to let at

E

lower rents. Such low-density building was naturally criticised and soon ceased. The money which Peabody, the American philanthropist, provided was therefore used, in the 1860s and onwards, for tall blocks. Since 1880 living in flats has become acceptable to wealthier classes, partly as a result of following the working-class example, but also by adopting for family life the London feature of apartments and chambers for single gentlemen which must go back to the Middle Ages.

Statistics about the number of rooms per family, the proportion of houses in 1900 without water closets, or those in 1960 without bathrooms, are one index to modern town life by which amenities unknown in the seventeenth century are now regarded as necessary to all. There is no similar body of statistics to reveal how fittings and furnishings in modern homes have changed, but some of the major developments are marked by technical inventions. One of them was wall-paper ⟨146⟩. In 1712 the government thought wall-paper popular enough to carry a tax, and so it did for over a hundred years, though at the end of the eighteenth century it was only used by the gentry, a few wealthy parsons and farmers and by professional people in the towns. Even the middle classes had no more than one or two rooms hung with it—the parlour and the best chamber over the parlour. Most people had only whitewashed walls. By 1800 printing with wood blocks and distemper colours began to oust flock and stencilled and hand-coloured papers, but the great revolution was caused early in the nineteenth century by the introduction of cylinder printing machines. The technical difficulties were so mastered by 1850 that prices fell considerably and wall-paper was much more widely used.

Floorcloth, as a cheap alternative to carpets, was in use from the eighteenth century. Shortly after 1800 a method was found of painting it or impregnating it with oil to make it easily cleaned and also resistant to damp, the chief problem in houses built before about 1850 without a damp course. The coating of canvas with a preparation of oxidised linseed oil was patented in the U.S.A. in 1860 under the name of linoleum, and by 1900 was to be found in better working-class homes. Oilcloth for the table was first manufactured in continuous lengths in 1804 but only became cheap after 1870.

Very few of the amenities now regarded as essential are more than a century old; they belong to the second phase of the Industrial Revolution, when technical developments began to be applied to the consumer market. The oil lamp was perfected in the 1840s, to burn vegetable or animal oil, or best of all turpentine, but only the invention after 1850 of processes for extracting paraffin from shale oil, and later from petroleum, brought oil lighting into widespread use. It also brought the oil heater, and into working-class homes paraffin candles to replace tallow candles. Gas for lighting in the home is no more than about a century old. The handyman of a generation or two ago had to be as ready to replace an incandescent gas mantle as he is now to renew a fuse. The blue flame burner was invented in 1855, and a gas cooker was shown in the Crystal Palace Exhibition of 1851, but gas cookers were not in general use until the twentieth century.

The products of the iron industry began to reach the home after 1800. A combined fireplace, boiler and cast-iron oven, complete with damper, is said to have been advertised in 1806, but the kitchen range certainly did not become common until the 1850s ⟨119⟩. The back boiler, a peculiarly British addition to the open fire, arrived in the 1870s. The mincing machine belongs to the 1860s, the cast-iron bath to about 1880. Enamel and galvanised wares were unknown until Victoria's reign.

Sir John Harrington invented the valve water closet in 1596, but it did not come into general use. 'Not a single patent for a water closet of any kind was taken out in the first 158 years of British patents (1617–1775)'[19], and the main technical improvements to it belonged to the years after 1870 ⟨215⟩. In any case such an amenity had to wait until a continuous piped water supply was generally available, and that has taken more than a century to achieve since the introduction of cast-iron water mains in 1810–20. Water closets were still the luxury of the few in many northern towns in 1900, and the smell of cess-pits or badly constructed drains was familiar to Victorian middle-class families. Fixed baths in a proper bathroom with running hot and cold water appear in wealthy homes about 1880 ⟨237⟩.

The catalogue of what the middle classes of 1850–1940 came to regard as essential could easily be extended—carpet sweepers and then vacuum cleaners; fabrics, and wall-papers fast-dyed so that they need not be shielded from the sun by drawn curtains; gas or electricity for cooking, heating and lighting. The one traditional feature of home life in this island that no class was ready to give up was the open fire. The middle-class home has had countless products of modern technology inserted into it but it has not, as a machine for living in, been redesigned. The explanation is easy to find. Home life is still, as it has always been, constructed round a framework of customary ways easily modified in detail but remarkably resistant to radical alteration.

Three factors enabled working-class families to make some headway in a society whose material standards were steadily rising. One was ability to improvise furniture, to make rugs, to hang wall-paper. 'Do it yourself' is not new, except as an advertiser's slogan. Fifty years ago a typical product was the snip rug on the hearth, made of small pieces of second-hand clothing (well washed) knotted through an open canvas; its general colour was the serviceable black or grey of Victorian men's clothing, with

E*

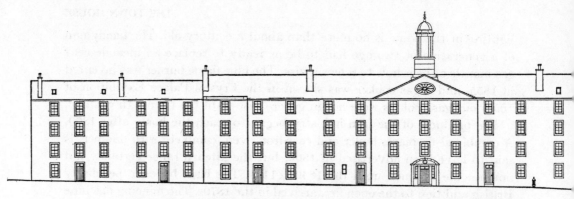

FIGURE 16. Weavers' tenements at New Lanark built by David Dale about 1785–90, long before Robert Owen's time. They are a fine expression of the way the Georgian tradition in architecture could be adapted to Scottish housing standards, and this group, with the three-storey building of the Lanark

a red diamond in the centre made from a soldier's tunic. Does any folk museum possess one? Another factor was the growth of an organised market in second-hand clothing and furniture. One aspect of the emergence of the welfare state is that in the last fifteen years the business of the pawn-broker, the second-hand clothing shop and the junk shop has dwindled. Still a third factor was the growth of credit trading. The tallyman, or packman, or 'Johnny-come-fortnight'—there must be even more local names for him—was the successor of the medieval chapman, travelling the towns and villages with his stock of haberdashery, mercery and drapery. The great growth of retail shops from the seventeenth century onwards did not put him out of business, but made him more ready to give his customers credit. Tailors with a regular country round, especially in Scot-land, were equally ready to give credit; the coming of the railway extended the range and scale of their business. Working-class self-help created not only the friendly society, the sick club or the pig club, but also the clothing club. By the last quarter of the nineteenth century furniture shops were ready to furnish, on extended credit, the parlour or the bedroom of a newly married couple with linoleum, piano, china cabinet, sofa, double bed or wash-stand.

The great rise in living standards, particularly in the past twenty years, has removed the menservants, and even the maids, from the upper- and middle-class homes into factories to make cars, cosmetics and all the other common necessities. The elaborate structure of upper-class life has col-lapsed, and very many great houses have become museums. The pattern of middle-class daily life, spread over morning room, dining room, drawing room and nursery, and perhaps study as well, has contracted. Kitchens are turned into kitchen-dining rooms, or drawing room and dining room are

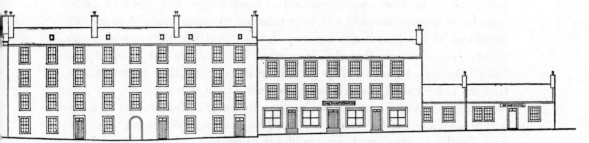

Provident Co-operative Society and the single-storey Post Office, embodies the whole range of Scottish tradition. The tenements also incorporate the ancient first-floor living tradition bequeathed by Scottish tower houses, for the ground-floor rooms are only wash-houses.

thrown into one. Indeed, what is fashionably called the 'open plan' is really the return home of an American emigrant of the seventeenth century: the hall living-and-eating room with the staircase rising from it. Changes in material standards and the decline of formality in social relations even threaten that peculiarly English shrine, the parlour. The one feeling common to all classes from the seventeenth century onwards was that visitors could not be formally entertained in the family's living room. Hence the peculiar status of the parlour in middle- and lower-class homes, once it was not needed as the principal sleeping room. It was in a sense the equivalent of the state rooms in a great house, but became more than that: it contained not only the best furniture but also family relics and valued objects; its window curtains and ornaments demonstrated the respectability of the family to the outer world; it was used only on Sunday (after dinner), when the habits and associations of the working life were inappropriate. The parlour was not the focus of family life, but its ideal: desired but, like many ideals, not really comfortable. Sociological study of modern housing has shown that rooms may not be used as the architect intended. Such discrepancies may easily be explained by the size of rooms or the way they are heated, but at the core of the matter is the simple fact that the family is completely at home only in one room. Strip away a variety of subsidiary factors—the needs of a man working at home, the desire for social status or the needs arising from social relations outside the family—and all that remains is the equation of one family with one hearth.

To fix the characteristics of housing conventions in this island at their sharpest, more detachment is needed than a native can easily assume. The Danish architect, S. E. Rasmussen, writing of London,[20] could see as peculiarities what an Englishman takes for granted: acceptance of house walls only 10 in. thick (not permitted in Copenhagen) or a positive preference for sash windows which it is impossible to make draught-proof. The reformers of the nineteenth century insisted that ventilation was a good thing because it was thought to prevent disease. Are our draughty, ill-heated houses a legacy of their good intentions or did they merely strengthen an older habit? Much more significant, though not necessarily more permanent, are the current preferences for certain features in the plan and arrangement of the house, and here England and Wales part company with Scotland, where customs are closer to continental ways. First in importance is the English preference, very deep-rooted and some would say ineradicable, for a separate dwelling for each family. That has made London what Rasmussen calls a scattered city, compared with concentrated cities such as Paris or Vienna; it has made every English town seem an unattainable ideal to foreign observers; it has created the garden city, and it eats up the countryside in a way that no government seems able or willing to stop. Nevertheless, the landscape of England's largest provincial cities, such as Newcastle, Leeds and Birmingham, has been revolutionised in the past ten years by the erection of blocks of flats as arresting in their scale as in their implications about the English way of life. Scotland has no need to make such a break with its past, for new flats are socially indistinguishable from old tenements ⟨239⟩.

The Englishman has come to expect his house to have more separate rooms than a foreigner wants, and especially more bedrooms. Rasmussen quotes a correspondent in the *Evening Standard* who was surprised to find that a four-room apartment in Copenhagen might have only one bedroom, and that the other three (smoking room, drawing room, dining room) each communicated with the other. The Englishman prefers his sitting room to have only one door, and certainly does not like rooms *en suite* or one bedroom reached only through another.

The common acceptance by those who build, or pay for building, of the separate dwelling with such ample accommodation compared with standards of other countries, has had two important consequences. The first is that the building industry, left to itself, proved unable to provide the housing required for the lower-paid section of the community. Hence building by local authorities of houses to let has made a contribution to the pattern of life here which is quite unparalleled elsewhere in scale or in kind ⟨234, 238⟩. Even so, municipal housing has failed to provide homes acceptable, in both economic and social terms, to a large section of the community. Hence that peculiarly English and especially depressing phenomenon, the house that has come down in the world: the Halifax weaver's house now turned into three cottages ⟨231⟩, or the large Georgian or Victorian house built by wealthy merchant or professional man and now divided into maisonettes, flats, tenements, or let as separate rooms to lodgers. This is no new problem. London must have had it in the Middle Ages, and Engels commented in 1844 on the Manchester families compelled to live in one room in a basement. Englishmen have shown more skill in creating homes, their 'castles', than in creating communities: the community of a block of flats, or a street of apartment houses with a row of shops on the ground floor. Perhaps in the next half-century we shall find new ways of achieving both these ends.

1 Madeline Kerr, *The People of Ship Street* (1958), 13–22.

2 J. T. Smith, 'Medieval Roofs: a classification', in *Archaeological Journal*, cxv (1958), 146 and figure 16.

3 *Testamenta Eboracensia* (Surtees Society), iii, 69, 125.

4 A. G. Leask, *Irish Castles* (Dundalk, 1951), 75.

5 J. T. Smith in *Chester Archaeological Society's Journal*, xlv (1958), 32–35.

6 *Testamenta Eboracensia*, ii, 23.

7 E. Estyn Evans, *Irish Folk Ways* (1957), 66.

8 S. H. Cruden, *Scottish Castles* (1960), chap. 5.

9 These paragraphs are based on the unpublished work of Mr. P. A. Kennedy on London inventories. I am much indebted to him for permission to make use of his material.

10 See G. R. Hibbard, 'The country house poem in the seventeenth century', in *Journal of the Warburg and Courtauld Institutes*, xix (1956), 159–74. The reference to the Duke of Chandos charging visitors to Cannons is quoted there from C. H. C. and M. I. Baker, *Life and Circumstances of James Brydges, First Duke of Chandos* (1949), 181.

11 C. Hussey, *English Country Houses: Early Georgian* (1955), 74.

12 J. Summerson, 'The Classical Country House in 18th Century England', in *Journal of the Royal Society of Arts*, cvii (1959), 551–52.

13 J. Summerson, *Georgian London* (1945), 50.

14 J. Summerson, *Architecture in England Since Wren* (1948), 29.

15 J. M. Richards, *Castles on the Ground* (1946), 9–10.

16 B. H. St. J. O'Neil, 'Bridge House, 64 George Road, Bermondsey, S.E.', in *Antiquaries Journal*, xxxii (1952), 192–97.

17 J. H. Clapham, *Economic History of Modern Britain*, ii (1932), 495.

18 F. Engels, *Condition of the Working Classes in England in 1844* (1943), 52–53.

19 L. Wright, *Clean and Decent* (1960), 71–75, 106.

20 S. E. Rasmussen, *London the Unique City* (1937), chaps. 10 and 12.

The history of the house as a house must be drawn from several distinct branches of study: archaeology and architectural history; economic history and topographical studies; social surveys. Much of the best and most recent work in the first group has been published in journals, either national, such as *The Archaeological Journal, Archaeologia* and *Medieval Archaeology*, or local. A bibliography of articles on smaller houses may be obtained from the Vernacular Architecture Group (Sir Robert de Z. Hall, Cross Farm, West Coker, Yeovil, Somerset). Apart from the many accounts of larger houses in *Country Life*, three volumes dealing with *English Country Houses* in the Georgian period have been compiled by Christopher Hussey. Sir John Summerson has produced analytical studies of large houses in *Architecture in Britain 1530–1830* (1950) and in *The Journal of the Royal Society of Arts*, cvii (1959). The county inventories of the three Royal Commissions on Historical Monuments, whose work is still in progress, contain descriptions of many thousands of houses, though until recently small houses have been summarily treated. Victoria County Histories, where new topographical volumes are still being produced, as in Warwickshire and Essex, contain accounts of vernacular building. The volumes of the Survey of London (especially the two produced in 1960 on *The Parish of St. James*) are most important for descriptions of surviving houses of all types. N. Lloyd's *History of the English House* (1949), his *History of English Brickwork* (1925) and R. Furneaux Jordan's *English House* (1959) are good pictorial histories of domestic architecture. D. MacGibbon and T. Ross, *The Castellated and Domestic Architecture of Scotland* (1887–92) is a masterpiece; S. H. Cruden's *Scottish Castles* (1960) provides a new general account of castles and tower houses. H. Taylor's *Old Halls in Lancashire and Cheshire* (1884) and L. Ambler's *Old Halls and Manor Houses of Yorkshire* (1906) are still very valuable. S. E. Rasmussen's *London the Unique City* (1937 and 1960) has stimulating chapters.

Good regional studies of farmhouses and cottages are as yet very rare. I. C. Peate's *The Welsh House* (1946) is a unique study of folk culture. Fox and Raglan's *Monmouthshire Houses* (three volumes, 1951–54) stands alone for its insight into the houses of one county. Other valuable regional surveys, such as those by C. F. Stell (the Halifax area), D. Portman (the Oxford region), P. Nuttgens (the north-east lowlands of Scotland), are as yet unpublished, but some are used in the writer's *The English Farmhouse and Cottage* (1961).

Some economic historians have included housing in their purview, notably Homans, *English Villagers of the Thirteenth Century* (1942), M. Campbell, *The English Yeoman* (1945). W. G. Hoskins has a section on peasant houses and interiors in *The Midland Peasant* (1957), M. Plant's *Domestic Life of Scotland in the Eighteenth Century* (1952) makes admirable use of contemporary material. Sir John Clapham's *Economic History of Modern Britain* (three volumes, 1926–38) also uses contemporary material, especially from county volumes produced by the Board of Agriculture in late Georgian times, and from Victorian Blue Books. S. Pollard, *History of Labour in Sheffield* (1960), has descriptions of working-class housing in Sheffield in the nineteenth century.

A most important documentary source consists of the many thousands of inventories of English and Welsh houses made, especially from *c.* 1575 to *c.* 1850, for purposes of probate. Some early series have been published, notably by the Surtees Society: *Testamenta Eboracensia, Wills and Inventories from the registry of the archdeaconry of Richmond* and *Wills and Inventories from the registry at Durham* (various dates).

BIBLIOGRAPHICAL NOTES

F. W. Steer's *Farm and Cottage Inventories of Mid-Essex, 1635–1749* (1950) is the only published series for a later period, though this material is used by W. G. Hoskins and by the writer in the works already cited.

Sociological studies which are relevant not only for present conditions and customs but also for their reflection on the past include M. W. Williams, *Social Survey of an English Village: Gosforth* (1956), A. D. Rees, *Life in a Welsh Countryside* (1951) and Dennis Chapman, *The Home and Social Status* (1955).

WITHDRAWN-UNL

1. The Bayeux Tapestry, woven within a few years of the Norman Conquest, whose story it relates, is a remarkable pictorial record. It contains accurate representations of many aspects of 11th-century society, including houses. This section shows Harold's manor house at Bosham, Sussex, where the hall was on the first floor, approached by an outside stair and over a vaulted or arcaded basement. This type of dwelling had a long life and an enduring influence on the housing tradition of this island, especially in Scotland.

2. A medieval undercroft in London House, High Street, Burford, Oxfordshire. The steps in the background show that it is only partly below street level, though the entrance from the street is now blocked. Such vaulted cellars were common in medieval towns, and have often survived the rebuilding of the houses above them.

3. Little Wenham Hall, Suffolk, is the best preserved 13th-century house in this country, and the earliest example of domestic building in brick. It is shown here because it is a first-floor hall house, as the window arrangement shows. The basement has a stone vault, and the low tower, which with the hall range makes an L plan, contains a chapel at first floor level with a chamber over it. The house was built c. 1270–80.

4. This section of the Bayeux Tapestry shows a foraging party, with cottages in the background. Their main features are unmistakable: an entrance in the centre of a side wall, no chimney (and probably no fire), a hipped roof. The walls appear to be of stone in one case and horizontal boards in the others, with roofs of stone, slate or wooden shingles.

5. The commonest type of house in the 13th century and onwards had, as its principal room, a large hall on the ground floor, open to the roof, and a storeyed extension at one end or both. In the Wealden type, the whole is under one continuous roof, as here at Link Farm, Egerton, Kent. The entrance is at the lower end of the hall. The hall has been divided into two storeys, but the sill and mullions of the original hall windows, running up to the eaves, can still be seen. The ground floor rooms at both ends are used for storage or similar purposes and the chamber at the farther end is the best in the house.

6. The hall roof is the oldest status symbol in the history of the house. At Great Dixter, Northiam, Sussex (15th century), the roof was bound to impress, either in the clear light of the tall windows, or at night, when the soaring beams were dimly lit by the open fire in the centre, but the same effect was just as eagerly sought in more modest houses.

7. Those who wanted more storage room downstairs got it by building wings at right-angles to the hall. In this farmhouse at Monks Eleigh, Suffolk, the relative height of the hall roof in relation to the wings shows that it was originally only one storey and open to the roof. The chimney is modern—and the fireplace to which it belongs.

8. An open medieval hall from the outside, with a storeyed solar block across its lower end. This house at Martock, Somerset, was built in the 14th century by the Treasurer of Wells Cathedral, who had a manor there. The roof covering of pantiles is modern, but the fine timber roof, renewed in the 15th century, is intact inside. There is no fireplace, so the hall must have been heated by an open hearth. The nearer of the two doorways is modern; the farther (original) doorway leads into the typical screens passage.

9. Wall fireplaces with a great hood and a chimney were usual in first-floor halls from the 12th century, although the stone vaulted roof of the basement might have taken a central hearth without damage. This fireplace at Luddesdown Court, Kent, is of 13th-century date and has a flat stone lintel composed of stones with joggled, or interlocking, joints.

10. A man warming himself at a fire was the usual subject for February in medieval sets of representations of the seasons. This one is from a church misericord at Screveton, Notts.; the man sits in an elaborately carved chair before a fireplace with a chimney hood, behind him a jug on a stool. These carvings suggest that to own one chair was not uncommon, even among medieval peasants.

11. The vast hall of Winchester Castle, indistinguishable in design and scale from a cathedral, was intended for ceremonial rather than domestic purposes. An open hearth in the centre of the floor was the most efficient way of heating such a room.

12.

An open hearth required an aperture or louvre on the ridge of the roof for the escape of smoke. From the louvre evolved the type of stone chimney shown here, at the medieval manor house of West Coker, Somerset. This chimney serves a gable-end fireplace, and was replaced later by one with a tall stack (and no doubt a narrower flue), giving a better draught.

13. The screens passage in Fir Tree Farm, Forncett St. Mary, Norfolk, built *c.* 1550; on the left the doorway into the hall, on the right two doorways (one of them now blocked) into two service rooms. Larger houses of earlier date often had three doorways, the central one leading by a passage between the service rooms to a kitchen beyond. The floor is laid with quarry tiles, of a design virtually unchanged from late medieval to recent times.

14. A significant division within 16th-century society lay between those who used an upper room in a wing as the best chamber or solar, and those on the other hand who used such a room merely for storage purposes. In this instance, from Alston Court, Nayland, Suffolk, the ceiling and fireplace prove that this can properly be called a solar. The furnishings are all later, though the warming pan may be noted as a common 17th- and 18th-century amenity.

15. Window seats like these in a chamber at the 14th-century Preston Patrick Hall, Westmorland, are a normal feature. They would certainly have cushions in the middle ages. The window was not glazed originally, but had double shutters, for the upper and lower half, and the hinges can still be seen. The upper half could be opened to admit light while the lower was kept shut to exclude draughts. The horizontal bar or transom is there to facilitate this division rather than to strengthen the mullion, as in large church windows. When window glass became cheaper, the upper half alone may have been glazed; such was certainly the practice in 16th-century Scotland.

16. The bay window appears for the first time in the later middle ages, in houses of good or superior quality. When it is found in the first floor room of a wing, as in this example at Church Farm, Parham, Suffolk, it denotes the solar, and is usually described as an oriel window. It is supported on stone corbels or a wooden bracket, often carved as here, and its head is often level with the eaves. In this instance the gable above is jettied, but the timber frame has been rendered over.

17. A medieval shop at Lavenham, Suffolk, with a double shop window, some of the woodwork of which has been renewed. Such shops sometimes had shutters hinged horizontally so that when dropped they served as counters, inside or out. The living rooms were entered through the shop, or by a back door.

18. Washing before and after meals in the middle ages meant using a jug and basin, either of which might be fixed near the slop stone shown here from the 14th-century Woodsford Castle, Dorset. The waste water was then thrown on to the sloping stone and found its way down the outside face of the wall. Such an amenity was only to be found in manor houses or other homes of similar status. These domestic sinks differ from the piscina in a church only in that, for liturgical reasons, the piscina has a soak-away in the thickness of the wall.

19. The stone drain at Plas Newydd, Cefn, Denbighshire. Such drains were common in remote parts of Western Europe—in farmhouses of Central France, in Irish tower houses, or in Yorkshire cottages—until recent times.

20. The South side of Vicars' Court, Lincoln, built *c.* 1310 for vicars choral of the Minster, viewed from the lower side, where there are three floors. The buttresses have, in modern times, had fireplaces and chimney flues cut in them. The large projections are garderobe towers, with small trefoil openings for ventilation on the top floor, and arched openings at ground level for cleaning.

21. The stone garderobe seat at Longthorpe Tower, Northants.—now lying on the floor of the garderobe.

22. Haddon Hall, Derbyshire, looking at the hall range which separates the lower and upper courts. Piecemeal development of this fortified manor house serves to epitomise much of the history of a great house. The lower (i.e. nearer) court was added in the 15th century, primarily to give lodgings to guests, to a classic example of 14th-century planning. Various minor improvements, such as making a gallery, took place in the Tudor period, and the whole was carefully restored in the 1920s.

23. Dartington Hall, Devon, showing part of the range of household lodgings which originally occupied two sides of the courtyard, flanking the hall built *c.* 1385–90 by John Holland, Duke of Exeter, half-brother of Richard II. The separate bed-sitting rooms were entered by pairs of doors under a porch (*right*), those on the first floor being entered by an outside stair which has gone. All the windows shown here are modern, as are the dormers. Each chamber had its privy or garderobe.

24.

The kitchen of a medieval house was normally detached from the house proper prior to the 15th century, and many such kitchens were built in the following two centuries. Medieval kitchens are now rare, either because they have been demolished or completely altered, or because they are in some cases indistinguishable from detached brewhouses. This grand kitchen at Glastonbury, belonging to the Abbot's Lodging there, is quite exceptional. It has four fireplaces, each set diagonally in a corner, with flues leading up to the louvre.

25.

The detached kitchen of the Vicarage at Exminster, Devon. The central doorway leads to the kitchen itself, the nearer one to the store chamber over; the nearer window is a modern insertion. It is probably of 15th-century date, and was described in 1679 as 'an old house built with stone and covered with reed, two parts (i.e. rooms) in the bottoms, one in the top, one oven to bake standing in the chimney, and place to brew'. Though such outbuildings were built as kitchens in the middle ages, they were used in later times, if at all, only for baking and brewing, and were still being built new for that purpose in Welsh towns in the 19th century.

26. A farmhouse near Cotton, Suffolk, surrounded by its medieval moat. Hundreds of manor houses, mainly in the English lowlands, had such a moat; it was as much a symbol of status as a precaution against attack. Other patches of water nearby may have been fishponds.

27. A farm building at Yardworthy in the Dartmoor parish of Chagford, Devon, which was built in the middle ages as a farmhouse. The porch consists of a few simply dressed pieces of granite, its roof of one flat slab. But for the enduring material, this building would have vanished long ago, as have all the houses of the poorer peasants.

28. The vicar's fortified house or pele, standing in the corner of the churchyard at Corbridge, Northumberland. It has a basement for storage, a hall on the first floor and a chamber on the second. The stairs go up in the thickness of the wall, in a narrow passage easily blocked or defended. Each room has a fireplace; there is an angled reading desk of stone by a window in the hall, and the corbelled-out chute of the garderobe in the chamber can be seen on the north wall (*above left*).

29. Affleck Castle (Angus) represents the kind of tower house built by a lesser laird in the second half of the 15th century: superb masonry (once harled or rendered over), simple plan, fairly elaborate internal arrangement. The turret houses the main stair as far as the hall level on the second floor, and has a small chapel in its top stage. The main block is vaulted, but in this instance at first floor level, with the hall over it. There is one chamber in the top storey. There is not much emphasis on defence from attack, but the internal arrangement is deliberately complicated to baffle the marauder.

30. The dairy in the ground floor of the 14th-century tower at Burneside Hall, Strickland Roger, Westmorland. The tower had two such chambers, with a vaulted passage between to a kitchen detached from the house. The room has no doubt always been used for this purpose, but it is now lighted by electricity, and the milk vessels are all of metal instead of wood. Note the great slate slabs, cool and easily cleaned. In the north midlands such a stone or brick shelf in buttery or dairy was known as the *brandreth*, in the midlands as the *gantry*, in East Anglia as the *stall*.

31. Borthwick (Midlothian) is one of the finest late medieval tower houses with its enclosure wall in Britain: built in 1430, completely unaltered and now happily restored and inhabited. On plan it consists of a rectangular block, with two wings on one side, making it possible to have hall, kitchen and one chamber all on the first floor. The walls are 12–14 ft. thick, and both basement and first floor are vaulted. The hall, shown here, has a fine hooded fireplace flanked by high window-openings like tunnels; the vault was plastered and painted with allegorical scenes. The doorway below the painting leads to a chamber; beyond it is a wall cupboard with gabled ornament over, also coloured originally.

32. The last generation of heads of religious houses lived very comfortably, and after the Dissolution any new set of lodgings, such as those built by the Prior of Watton, a Gilbertine house in the East Riding of Yorkshire, was likely to be taken over as a private house. The fine storeyed oriel lighted a hall on the ground floor and the prior's dining-chamber over it. The top floor, reached by a newel stair in the turret, consisted of one large room, no doubt a dormitory either for guests or for the prior's servants.

53. Barrington Court, Somerset, built *c.* 1530. When storeyed houses became more common, the staircase was an essential element in the design. The principle of the turret or wing containing a newel staircase was taken over from the castle and the monastery for domestic building. In grand houses, such as this, there are often two staircases in the angles between the hall block and the wings, to balance the design. Barrington Court is also one of the earliest examples of a symmetrical front with a porch making an E-plan.

34.

In smaller houses such as this at Otley, Suffolk, the vernacular builder did not attempt to make the staircase wing an architectural feature, but placed it at the rear of the hall wing. Since his material was timber, the design could scarcely be other than rectangular on plan, but masons in the highland zone using rubble stone and builders of cob houses in the West Country often built a round projection. In the 17th century, such large wings as this became more common, since a framed staircase took more space than a simple spiral stair.

35. The dog-leg type of staircase fitted into a rectangular space. The timber framework—newel posts, strings and rails—are usually of substantial proportions and moulded. The country carpenter could not always produce turned balusters, and then fitted flat ones such as these in Hergest Court, Kington, Herefordshire (*below left*).

36. The well type of staircase filled a square space. These early staircases had very solid newel posts, sometimes (as here) continued up to the next flight, hand rails and strings, with substantial balusters, usually turned. When this staircase was inserted, *c.* 1700, in Preston Lodge, Cupar, Fifeshire, its design was rather old-fashioned by English standards.

37. The west range at Gainsborough Old Hall, Lincolnshire, providing twelve sets of identical chambers for servants of the household, each with its fireplace and garderobe. Such provision can also be seen at Dartington Hall, Devon (*c.* 1390), and at Haddon Hall, Derbyshire (late 15th century); the great gatehouse at Layer Marney, Essex (*c.* 1520) served the same purpose, and in the great houses of Elizabeth's time the ranges flanking a courtyard were similarly arranged, either for guests or for the household.

38. We are so familiar with great country houses that it is impossible for us to realise how new a house like Wollaton Hall, Nottinghamshire, was when Sir Francis Willoughby finished it in 1588—how novel in its scale, its design and its details. It has been called a piece of pure extravagance; its designer, Robert Smythson, has been credited with wishing to give it the romantic look of a medieval castle. Whatever the explanation, it belongs to the earliest group of houses built to impress the eye and the imagination of the beholder. It incorporated one portentous novelty of plan: kitchens and other services in the basement, actually above ground level but very ill-lit.

39. Fyvie Castle, Aberdeenshire, is the most fantastic product of Scottish baronial architecture. This front is mainly Elizabethan in date; the great towers and turrets make a fine martial show, but the result is pure poetry, not military strength. Sir Alexander Seton, who created the new elevation, had studied in Rome and in France, and there is certainly French influence here. Here the service rooms on the ground floor are a legacy from medieval tradition; not, as at Wollaton, an innovation.

40. By the 16th century, the Scottish laird required more rooms in his tower house, and Claypotts (Angus), built in 1569, is a superb example of the Z plan which was very popular at the time. It consists of a central block with a round tower at opposing angles, and a stair turret tucked in between; it combines efficient ideas of defence (note the gunports on the ground floor, one of them in the kitchen fireplace!) with a deliberate search for romantic effect. There are four floors. The ground floor contains a kitchen and stores; the hall is on the first floor, with two other rooms in the towers; the two top floors each have three rooms. The top stage is crowded with characteristically Scottish features; corbelled angles, crow-stepped gables, and a dormer with Renaissance ornament.

41. Cranborne Manor, Dorset, is a medieval hunting lodge, bought by Robert Cecil, Earl of Salisbury, in 1600 and then renovated and enlarged to make it suitable for grand entertaining. The original hall (situated on the first floor with a kitchen fitted into the medieval undercroft below) had its walls covered with oak wainscotting and tapestries; only the thickness of the walls reveals the age of the building.

42.
In the 16th century, the demand for comfort led to the building, in superior houses, of internal or wind porches inside private rooms. The earliest are about 1530, and they were fashionable for about a century, especially in southern and south-western counties. This porch is in what was originally a parlour at Cotehele House, Calstock, Cornwall.

43. The partition between hall and parlour in a mid-Tudor farmhouse in the West Country: Bartonbury, Down St. Mary, Devon. Such internal divisions were commonly of timber in stone houses, and care was given to their finish. This one is constructed of vertical studs, chamfered at the edges down to the level of the fixed bench, with planks between; the studs are tenoned into a sill beam on the ground and into a very substantial moulded beam at the top which also supports the joists of the hall ceiling. The beam is plain on the parlour side, showing the room had less social standing than the hall. The house had cobbled floors throughout until early in this century, and the cream oven beyond the sideboard on the left of this view is shown in plate ⟨120⟩.

44. A cruck-built house at Lacock, Wilts. Good stone is available locally, but this and other houses in it show that timber-framed building was a significant part of the local vernacular until the 16th century, and that stone walls with slate roofs represent the 17th and early 18th century methods of building. Bricks were later made nearby, as is shown by some of the filling of this gable. The dormer window is no doubt 18th or 19th century, for this house was certainly open to the roof originally.

45. In the west midlands, the carpenter had no competition from the stonemason and created his finest houses. Preston Court in West Gloucestershire is a manor house built more like a town house, with its great jettied and gabled second floor. The roomy garrets were required in this sheep farming country for storing farm produce; one of them still contains a wooden hoist for lifting sacks of wool, another a set of hanging shelves, designed to ripen cheeses and to defeat the mice.

46. The pride of the owner of a new house of the 16th or 17th century is shown in the rather insolent inscription on a beam of this house at Madeley, Staffordshire: 'Walk, knave. What look'st at? 1647'. The house is, incidentally, a good example of the style of building in timber in the west midlands. The part on the right is a storeyed porch.

47. In the prodigy houses of late Elizabethan times, a great display was made of traditional features such as the screen in the hall. This is the screen from Burton Agnes Hall, East Yorkshire, surmounted by tiers of allegorical plaster reliefs.

48. The long gallery at Astley Hall, near Chorley, Lancashire, with contemporary furniture. The house was rebuilt *c.* 1670 in stone and brick, replacing a timber house, in a style then old-fashioned by a generation or more. The long gallery occupies the whole of the first floor front, and is continuously glazed on three sides in a manner first seen in late Elizabethan houses like Hardwick. In the 17th century the indoor games of billiards and shuffleboard became popular among the upper classes, and here is an original shuffleboard table. The 18th-century indoor game of bowls, using glazed pottery balls, was no doubt also played in long galleries.

50. Although every new farmhouse and most old ones had a chamber over the hall by 1700, that room did ▶ not readily become part of the purely human part of the household routine. Any upper room in a farmhouse was likely to be used for storage purposes, especially the chamber over the hall, both because it was a new feature and because it was the warmest and driest. The warmth from the hall below easily spread upwards when the floorboards were not underdrawn with plaster. This chamber at Stanton's Farm, Black Notley, Essex, built over an aisled hall whose upper structure is clearly seen, was still used as a store in this century; it has now been tidied up.

49.

Most new houses of the 16th century were built with a chamber over the hall, and in old houses such a chamber could be inserted. Evidence of this new fashion can be seen in hall ceilings, such as this from the Ancient House Museum, Thetford, Norfolk. The main beams are moulded, and so are the joists, which have very elaborate stops at their junction with the beams. Ceilings were rarely underdrawn with plaster prior to the 17th and 18th centuries, except in superior houses such as that shown in ⟨77⟩.

51. A comparison of this Essex farmhouse, Gray's Farm, Chignall, with ⟨7⟩ will show how a medieval farmhouse could be modernised by 17th-century standards. It also shows the external effect of the change shown in ⟨50⟩. The hall block was raised a full storey, without altering the 15th-century wings; at the same time a chimney stack was inserted for the fireplaces of the hall and the chamber over it. A new staircase was also put in, some new windows in the front of the house, and wainscotting in a parlour.

52. A ceiling of similar quality to that from Thetford ⟨49⟩, when found in the ground-floor room of a wing rather than in the hall, shows that the room is a parlour, and not merely a service room or store-room. This is the Elizabethan parlour ceiling at Bodidris, Llandegla, Denbighshire; it was no doubt the best bedroom originally, but later became the dining-room.

53 & 54.

A chamber at Fir Tree Farm, Forncett St. Mary, Norfolk, and ⟨54⟩ the hall at Maenan, Caernarvonshire. Plaster ceilings were a new way of making rooms draught-proof. They were first done by Italian craftsmen, in the Tudor period, and became a principal vehicle of Renaissance ornament—even applied, in ⟨54⟩, to the arched bosses and purlins of a medieval roof. In ⟨53⟩ the chamber has a closet with a ventilation opening above the door filled with turned spells. In front of the fireplace stands an 18th-century clothes press.

55. The cheapest form of wall decoration was painted cloths; in the years 1575–1640 even the village labourer living in a two-roomed house commonly possessed them. They consisted of canvas stretched on a wooden frame; painters or stainers must have travelled round the countryside making them. They are now so rare that we do not know how often they were pictorial, how often merely stencilled patterns. This example, one of a set now in the Luton Museum, shows the ascension of Elijah (2 Kings, ii, 11–14); Elisha (left centre) stands by the Jordan, while the chariot drawn by horses of fire carries off Elijah and his mantel falls in the centre of the panel. The subject illustrates well the religious interests of the middle and lower-middle classes in the early 17th century. (*See sketch below.*)

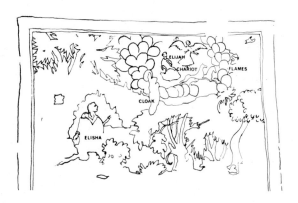

56. Wall paintings of the 16th and 17th centuries are consciously substitutes for tapestry. They often have a frieze of Renaissance design, with pictures below; the gentry favoured classical or allegorical themes, the middle classes Biblical topics. Here is a secular subject at West Stow, Suffolk: a youth hawking ('Thus do I all the day'), a young man courting ('Thus do I while I may'), a married man envious ('Thus did I when I might') and an old man leaning on a stick ('Good Lord, will this world last for ever?').

57. Cheaper paintings consisted simply of stencilled patterns, as in this fragment from Stamford, Lincolnshire. One of the last manifestations of the fashion, early in the 18th century, imitates panelling.

58. This sad picture, taken at Yaxley, Huntingdonshire, in 1957, shows that even quite modest houses in south-eastern England might have painted wall plaster—in this instance in a chamber ceiled over at purlin level.

59. In 17th-century Scotland, the plastered ceiling was rare, but paint could be applied to open joists and the underside of floorboards, as well as to plastered walls. Gladstone's Land, Lawnmarket, Edinburgh, has this room with an arcaded design on the walls, each opening filled with an urn and flowers; the joists and boards have panels containing floral ornament.

60 & 61.

Those who built new houses or improved old ones were singularly proud of their work: witness the new fashion for date stones such as that over the door of a barn at Long Lee, Rowarth, Derbyshire ⟨60⟩, or in the pediment of a window at Tal-y-llyn, Llanbeulan, Anglesey ⟨61⟩.

62, 63, 64 & 65.

Glazed windows became a common feature in all but the poorest houses in the period 1575 onwards, and were obviously a source of pride as well as comfort. The mullions were modified in section to facilitate glazing, and when loftier openings were required, a horizontal transom was put in to strengthen the mullions. ⟨62⟩ A window at Cerrig-y-Drudion, Denbighshire, with medieval type mullions, of oak and diamond-shaped in section, used in the new type of opening with a transom. ⟨63⟩ A window with round-headed openings in stone at Abergele, Denbighshire; it is dated 1585. ⟨64⟩ A mullioned window of Cotswold type in a storeyed porch at Stow-on-the-Wold, Gloucestershire, dated 1615. Such windows could be fitted with a hinged iron casement. ⟨65⟩ A larger window of similar date in the manor house at Brantingby, Leicestershire.

66–9. Chimneys were an even more powerful symbol of status than windows, and Charles II's government was acute enough to see that hearths could be a useful source of revenue; people would rather pay tax than give them up, just as modern man puts up with taxes on tobacco, beer and petrol. To make a chimney stack as imposing as possible the chimneys were divided, or made to look more numerous than they were by a zig-zag profile. In the west country the stack was often built by the front door, of contrasting materials. There are even 18th-century cottages with a false stack. ⟨66⟩ Divided chimneys on a brick manor house at Leverington, Cambridgeshire. ⟨67⟩ Separate octagonal chimneys at Monks Eleigh, Suffolk, with the date 1658 and the owner's initials. ⟨68⟩ A typical chimney in Flintshire, Ty Isaf at Hendre. ⟨69⟩ A cottage built at Stickney, Lincolnshire, about 1800; the farther stack is a dummy.

70. Although chimneys were now much more common, as William Harrison commented in 1577, some rooms, such as the parlour of an Elizabethan house, were often unheated. Hence, houses like Hunt Street Farm, Crundale, Kent, may have had chimneys added at any date from the 17th century onwards.

71. Raynham Hall, Norfolk, built in 1635, shows even more clearly than Wollaton Hall ⟨38⟩ how the basement floor, with its kitchens, etc., was lighted, and also what view the servants got from their bedrooms in the garrets.

72. Service in a gentleman's household or else a farmhouse was the usual lot of village girls; they took their meals, if it was a large household, in the servants' hall, often a basement room. There, rank and discipline were carefully observed, with the butler and housekeeper taking meals at a small table, the rest at one of the long tables. Elsewhere in the basement was the kitchen, with its great ranges and long deal tables, a gloomy place when the voices and movement have gone. The servants' hall at Chirk Castle, Denbigh.

73.

At the top of three or more flights of stairs were the garrets where servants slept; whitewashed and wholesome but comfortless. These garrets are in Cotton Hall, Denbigh (compare ⟨ 123 ⟩).

74. Cawdor Castle, Nairnshire, is a large courtyard castle, the whole complex still dominated by the great 15th-century tower keep. Round it are three courtyards, almost entirely surrounded by buildings added between the 16th and the 19th centuries. The principal remodelling took place in the second half of the 17th century, and included linking the keep with the hall in the right-hand block, and also providing a wide square staircase.

75. Kellie Castle, Fifeshire, may have had a courtyard originally, but if so later building has covered it, probably in the Elizabethan period when the building assumed its present form. The first floor is the living level; the kitchen is in the basement. The principal entrance is into the left-hand tower, but from first-floor level the spiral staircase rises in the corbelled-out turret in the angle. Scottish window openings, including dormers, have characteristically long proportions. There is nothing military about Kellie Castle—no gun ports, and no hesitation about windows facing outwards.

76.

This house in Elie, Fifeshire (once a fishing port, now a seaside resort), is known as the Castle, but there is nothing military about it. Built perhaps early in the seventeenth century, it is clearly a first floor house; the basement is vaulted. It incorporates a modest tower on the left, and the entrance is on the farther side of the staircase wing in the foreground.

77.

Great Addington Hall, Northamptonshire: the type of 17th-century manor house characteristic of the limestone belt. The design is medieval, modified but recognisable. Hall and cross wings have two storeys with garrets. The porch is placed centrally, for symmetry, and has the effect of making the hall no more than an entrance lobby, though it has a fireplace. There are later wings on each side, and some windows have been lengthened.

78.

In the great rebuilding of 1575–1640, the commonest type of farmhouse in the west had three rooms and a cross passage, but with two storeys throughout. Examples can be diagnosed from outside by the relation of doorway, windows and chimneys. In this house, White's Farm, South Hart, South Petherton, Somerset, the nearest room is the kitchen. Then comes the cross passage, with the hall fireplace backing on to it, and at the farther end the parlour.

79.

In the seventeenth century the manorial monopoly of dovecotes (for the sake of their manure) collapsed, and hundreds of new dovecotes were built by farmers. They are usually free-standing, but occasionally, as here at Aynho, Northamptonshire, are incorporated in the house.

80 & 81.

By the 17th century the storeyed bay window, derived from the lofty oriel window of the early Tudor period, was being put into farmhouses, such as ⟨80⟩ from Chidding-fold, Kent, and into merchants' houses in towns. Examples in stone, such as ⟨81⟩ from Stamford, Lincolnshire, dated 1663, are such a feature of the limestone belt that they must have been made to pattern in the quarries, along with mullioned windows and doorways.

82. In almost every region the craftsmen engaged in house building and furnishing have at some time found a particularly vigorous form of expression. In East Anglia it was the carpenter's turn in the 16th century—witness the ceilings in ⟨49⟩—but by the 17th century timber was too scarce and poor in quality to give him an outlet. The plasterer took over, particularly after 1660, and finished his protective rendering of the timber frame of the house with an ornamental scheme, derived, either closely or remotely, from the patterns fashionable for internal work. Pargeting at Sibton, Suffolk.

83. This design was very popular in the west midlands from Elizabethan times for a century or more: a hall range with one cross wing. The hall range may contain hall alone, or, as in Baxter's House, Eaton Constantine, Salop, a hall with a kitchen or service rooms. The entrance is in the angle between hall and wing, and one chimney stack efficiently takes flues from three rooms. The wing may contain either two parlours, or one parlour with a buttery behind it.

84. It has sometimes been claimed that houses built with a gable end to the street (as here at Barrowby, Lincolnshire) are the oldest in the village. It is more likely that they represent infilling of the 16th and 17th centuries. They very often present a blank wall to the street but this example shows the symmetrical arrangement of windows favoured by masons, and the well-lighted garret, of that period.

85. Almshouses like these at Brackley, Northamptonshire (1633), provide in most regions of England the oldest surviving examples of rows of uniform housing. They are therefore a link between medieval rows—Vicar's Close, Wells ⟨*The Town*, 6⟩, or examples at York and Coventry probably built as an investment by religious institutions—and the terrace housing of modern times. This group illustrates an innovation of this age: external divisions no longer correspond to internal, for the chambers are half in the roof.

86.
By the end of the 17th century the protruding staircase wing went out of fashion; builders became more enterprising, especially when the client wanted a fairly large farmhouse, more than a simple row of rooms. This large farmhouse at Sutton Bonington, Nottinghamshire, built in the late 17th century, is typical of its age and region in having two lofty storeys throughout and large garrets, each stage marked by an ornamental string course. The windows breaking the string on the street side light the staircase, for which room has been found in the middle of the main range.

87. What Sir Roger Pratt, the gentleman architect of the 17th century, called 'the double pile' became popular in the midlands for small manor houses from *c.* 1675 to 1725. It was square on plan, and so gave the compactness impossible with traditional plans. The roof had two pitches and care had to be taken to get rid of water from the valley between. Bulcote Manor, Nottinghamshire, has a modern porch and some windows renewed. The string courses, ornamental in origin, indicate the height of ceilings, for the ledges so formed supported the joists.

88. The Devonshire long house had, by the end of its long history, separate doorways, side by side, into the cross passage (now become part of the house) and into the byre. This is Uppacott, Widecombe-in-the-Moor; the byre still has its stalls and drain, and is used in hard winter weather. The building is probably late 17th century in date.

89. The hearth fireplace backing on to the passage is shown in this photo of Lower Tor, in the same parish, built in 1707, and now not regularly inhabited.

90. In the Devonshire 'front chimney' house, the large fireplace had a small fire window in the corner near the front door, from which visitors could be espied. Tudor Cottage, Thorverton, Devon.

91. In Wales the nucleated village is unknown, and while midland farmers and labourers still crowded their houses together, the Welsh crofter built his *tyddyn* or small homestead where he had land and close to the moors where his sheep grazed. Many of these are now abandoned, mainly owing to the consolidation of land in the 19th century. Tan-y-Craig, Llangynog, Montgomery.

92 This Welsh crofter's cottage, Yr Gegin Fawr, Pant Glas Uchaf, Caernarvonshire, is an excellent
& example of its type; it is probably 17th century in date, consists of one room with a chamber over,
93. built of rubble stone with very substantial woodwork. There is a large hearth fireplace at the gable
end, flanked by a stone newel staircase in the thickness of the wall. The joists are slotted into the ceiling
beam so that they could be removed if required (before the ceiling was underdrawn), to take upstairs
furniture or stores too large for the staircase. It has been lovingly restored and furnished with local
antiques, such as the Caernarvonshire dresser; they may be somewhat superior to the original status
of the house, but they serve to underline the contrast, typical of the highland zone, between simple
standards and fine craftsmanship.

94. In Wales, the modernisation of medieval single-storey houses began, as it did in England, in the second half of the 16th century. Old houses had an upper storey inserted, new wings were added, and both these improvements can be seen at Bryn-ffanigl Ganol, Abergele, Denbighshire. The old range, on the right, now has a chamber over the hall (to the left of the chimney stack) and another over the third room beyond the passage.

95 &
96. In parts of Wales, particularly Pembrokeshire, fireplaces were often built out on a side wall, making a hearth space like the 'ingle neuk' in stone houses in the Scottish lowlands. The circular chimney stack may be a legacy of Norman colonisation of the county. ⟨95⟩ House at Jameston, Pembrokeshire. ⟨96⟩ Cerrig-y-Drudion, Denbighshire.

97. The West Yorkshire hill farm, commonly of 17th-century date, is one of the most characteristic houses to be found anywhere in the island, standing at 800 feet or more above sea level, linked with the roads only by its own track. Many have been abandoned since 1875; others have been purchased by local authorities constructing reservoirs, and their inhabitants evicted to ensure the purity of the water.

98. Royds Hall, Bradford, built during the Civil War, is characteristic of the region and age: low proportions under a rather low-pitched roof; a plan two rooms deep, and very large windows, especially in the hall (twelve lights in three groups of four, with a transom).

99.

The storeyed porch remained fashionable in middle-class houses. The porch of Scosthrop Manor, Airton, West Yorkshire, was added in 1686 to an older house.

100. Horton Old Hall, Bradford (1674). Even at this date, some West Riding houses were still built with a hall the full height of the house. A wooden gallery was then inserted to link the rooms upstairs in the wings.

101. In Yorkshire and other northern counties, the mason let himself go on doorways and fireplaces. At High Bentley, in the township of Shelf on the moors above Halifax, there are two coats of arms above a fireplace with a wavy lintel (the royal arms and a family coat, dated 1661). This is one of the many old houses in this region now uninhabited: in 1961 this hall was occupied only by young turkeys.

102. Parlour fireplace in Horton Old Hall, Bradford, inscribed as a memorial to Isaac and Susannah Sharp, 1675. Both this and ⟨103⟩ have cast-iron ranges inserted about 1800.

103. Fireplaces in chambers became much more common in the 17th century, though it is doubtful if they were used except in cases of illness. This fireplace at Coed y Cra Uchaf, Northop, Flintshire, is narrower than would be found in a hall or kitchen. The stonework has been blackened to match the iron range.

104. The new village schools of the 16th and 17th centuries usually had a school house under the same roof. This grammar school at Burnsall in the West Riding was founded in 1605, and has the master's house at the end.

105.

Collinfield, a small manor house at Kendal, Westmorland, has a 17th-century dog gate at the head of the stairs made, like the balustrade, of flat pierced balusters. Such gates are a common feature in farmhouses of this and the next century.

106. Spinning gallery, Crosthwaite, Westmorland. These galleries in Lake District farmhouses have excited interest and speculation. The facts are that only fourteen instances are recorded, all in the Lake District; none is earlier than the 17th century, nearly all face north, and if they were designed as places for women to sit and spin, direct sunshine was undesirable.

107. Causeway Farm, Windermere, was built about 1650, at an early stage of the great rebuilding in the Lake District. The hall still has its flagged floor and some of the fittings typical of this age: the long table, and the two-stage cupboard (dated 1661) built into the timber partition between hall and parlour.

108.

The merchants of King's Lynn adopted from the gentry of East Anglia and Lincolnshire the idea of a lofty brick tower, so that they could watch their vessels coming up the River Ouse. Here is the only surviving tower, behind a wealthy merchant's house in Queen Street; it contains a staircase, and rooms used no doubt for servants.

109.

In Edinburgh the problem of space in the old town below the castle was more acute than in London, and so building went higher. This tenement off the High Street was built early in the 17th century. The round staircase turret of these early tenements was taken over from the tower house, and the crow-stepped gables are another persistent vernacular feature.

110. London's answer to growing pressure on housing in the early 17th century was to build four-storey sky-scrapers in timber, such as this house at the corner of Chancery Lane. It is constructed in the traditional manner, with a jetty at each floor, but the ornament is entirely in the Renaissance idiom.

111. From the 17th century onwards, baking bread at home became general, and even cottages, such as this at Great Casterton, Rutland, had a deep oven built within the hearth, with a round or rectangular projection outside. This is a non-parlour type of cottage; the doorway at one end of a side wall, placed so that on entering one turns round a speer or screen at the side of the fireplace, is common in areas of stone building. Notice also the well in the garden, with a windlass.

112. This two-roomed cottage, mud-walled, at Aslockton, Nottinghamshire, is no older than the 18th century, but is a rare survival of a type once common in the midlands. There are two rooms, house and parlour (bedroom), and the last occupant described it as 'very snug' as he moved into a council bungalow. The brick addition on the left is a wash-house, with an earth closet in it.

113. Cottage at Stonesby, Leicestershire. The typical 18th-century cottage was one and a half storeys, with rooms upstairs entirely in the roof space, and so lit either by windows in the gables (as in ⟨117⟩), or by dormers. The design of the dormers depended on the roofing material; this type is the most convenient with pantiles.

114. In south-eastern England the mansard roof, with a pitch in two slopes to make more headroom upstairs, was widely adopted for middle-class houses with servants' rooms in the roof space. From towns like Stamford, Wisbech and King's Lynn it even spread to the adjacent villages. This is a cottage at Tydd St Mary's in the Lincolnshire Fens, with tumbled gables in the local manner. The upper storey was in this instance used originally for storage—hence the blocked door.

115. One of the major innovations of modern times is semi-detached housing. It appears sporadically in the eastern counties in the later 18th century. These cottages at Holbeach Clough, Lincolnshire, are dated 1793.

116. In the highland zone, the tradition of single-storey dwellings persisted through the 18th century; the principal variations were in the method of building, the number of rooms and windows, the type of hearth, and of course in the social status of the occupants. This cottage at Buckley, Flint, has four rooms, as many as a minister would have in a remote part of the Scottish Highlands, or a small farmer in north Wales.

117. A cottage on the waste at Honington, Salop. It is of Severn Valley type, with a large chimney stack built out at the gable end. The cottage stands on the verge of a main road, with the hedgerow behind it, but modern 'improvements' have spoiled any picturesque effect with the kerbed footpath and the concrete posts and wire fence.

118. In 18th-century Wales, long houses remained in use and new ones were built. Cilewent, Dyffryn Claerwen, Radnorshire, is a cruck-framed house, with the date 1734 over the lintel; it has a common entrance in the centre to the house part and cow-byre, and another entrance at the left to the stable. This house has since been taken down and re-erected in the Welsh Folk Museum, St Fagan's.

119.

The living-room or hall in Drawwell Farm, Lyth, Westmorland, has altered little since *c.* 1900, and some of its features are much older. The round-topped table was for the farmer and his family, the long table for the servants. The shelf under the ceiling may once have held oat cakes. The iron range with a baking oven on one side and a water-boiler on the other (notice the tap) may be *c.* 1860, not so old as the well-burnished steel crane from which the kettle hangs. The carpet in the background covers a treadle sewing machine, no doubt made by Singer, *c.* 1900. The embossed and painted tins on the mantelpiece have a Victorian look, and the illustrated calendars presented by shopkeepers in the market town have changed little in fifty years.

120.

Devonshire cream is enjoyed by thousands who have never thought how it is made. The cream is heated until it clots, and here is a cream oven—perhaps of 18th-century date—in Bartonbury, Down St. Mary. It is in the hall, the only room where there was always a fire from which a pan full of hot embers could be taken. The oven (if such it can be called) was made by cutting back the splay of the window; the cloam (earthenware) pan of cream stood over the embers placed in the opening below; there was no flue and ashes fell on the floor.

121.

The Renaissance idea of a symmetrical façade for a small manor house did no more than modify the internal arrangement at first. In this house at Fulbeck, Lincolnshire (about 1700), there are two rooms in the front, hall and parlour, and the entrance door leads directly into the hall, which thus occupies three-fifths of the frontage.

122.

During the course of the 18th century the two rooms in the front were separated from an entrance hall; fireplaces backing on the passage fitted perfectly the new fashion for a hipped roof. This house, at Widmerpool, Nottinghamshire, is on the frontier of the region to the south-east in which hipped roofs became general in the first half of the 19th century.

123.

A substantially-built old house, too good to pull down, could be given a new look. Cotton Hall, Denbighshire, has 1713 in the pediment over the front door and is completely Georgian in detail, but the design looks sub-medieval, and the chimney stacks, of early Jacobean character, show what has happened.

124. The change to brick building in the later 17th century and onwards was accompanied by a revolution in the proportions of houses. The bricklayer was obviously very confident of his ability to put up much loftier houses, and in particular to give his customers bedrooms with plenty of headroom. Buildings such as this at Llanerfyl, Montgomeryshire, could be paralleled in many midland counties and even in Somerset, a county of stone houses.

125. In Scotland, the owner of an old tower house could only build alongside it. At Bonshaw Tower, Dumfriesshire, the distance between the two suggests a growing contempt for the old.

126 & 127. The garrets of 18th-century farmhouses had to be made into usable bedrooms for servants. In some early Georgian houses the dormer windows are almost hidden behind a parapet ⟨126⟩: Underdown Farm, Eddington, Kent. Later, there was no attempt to hide them, and their height in the roof, compared with earlier dormers, shows how lofty bedrooms and garrets were required to be ⟨127⟩: house at Bledington, Gloucestershire.

128 & 129. In stone and brick houses of 1675 to 1750, especially in the midlands and north, a characteristic improvement is a closet alongside the gable-end fireplace, lighted by a small round window. Estate agents nowadays would call them powder closets; they may have been used as a conveniently closed space in which to powder a wig, or for clothes storage. ⟨128⟩ Bull's-eye windows in Manor Farm, Steeple Aston, Oxfordshire; ⟨129⟩ closets in Southwood Hall, Cottingham, East Yorkshire. The latter house has a panelled overmantel, and 'a principal compartment raised over it to receive a picture', as Isaac Ware recommended in his *Complete Body of Architecture* (1756).

130. A new type of house appeared in Scotland shortly before 1700: symmetrical in appearance, with fireplaces at the gable ends, and a full two storeys, but with only two rooms on a floor. It was suitable for merchants in coastal ports, for lesser lairds, tacksmen and farmers, and for the clergy. Key House, Falkland, is dated 1713 (*below*).

131. In the northern counties some large Jacobean houses have a lofty window lighting the staircase. In the 18th century this staircase window becomes a common feature of quite small houses. Cold Weather House, Nelson, Lancashire.

132. In open-field England, new farmhouses were built away from the village on ring-fence farms allotted at the enclosure. The open fields of Winteringham, Lincolnshire, were enclosed in 1798; this farmhouse, on the Humber side a mile from the village, bears a panel with: Play, pray and sing God save the King 1798.

133.

The country parson, if he could afford to rebuild his parsonage house, often showed that he knew the fashions, or could choose a builder with the most up-to-date pattern books. Hence the drawing-room wing at Offchurch Vicarage, Warwickshire, with its bowed end and sash windows down to the ground.

134.

All round the east and south-east coasts, and far into the east midlands, Dutch ideas in brick building were fashionable from 1660 to 1740. This curved Dutch gable is in Middle Street, Deal, Kent.

135. Air view of Blenheim Palace, Woodstock, Oxon., built by a grateful nation for the Duke of Marlborough and designed by Vanbrugh. Blenheim is the grandest example in this island of Baroque architecture. Its scale is colossal: the mass of the principal apartments is flanked by a stable court (*right*) and a kitchen court (*left*). To the great families of the 18th century, only such immense (and to us, impractical) houses were proper to their status and way of life.

136. The entrance hall at Syon House, Isleworth, Middlesex, a Tudor house, on the site of a medieval nunnery, altered by Robert Adam (1761) for the first Duke of Northumberland. The hall was now merely a foretaste in architecture of the splendour of the great house—in this case a polished stone floor, marble columns with gilt capitals topped by antique statuary, and mahogany doors.

137. Houghton Hall, Norfolk, is an outstanding example of one of the great country homes of the Whig oligarchy who ruled early Georgian England. A contemporary said it was 'the best house in the world for its size, capable of the greatest reception for company and the most convenient State apartments, very noble, especially the hall and saloon.' Here is the saloon, finished in 1731, predominantly in gold and crimson, marble and mahogany.

138. Alongside the saloon, and often communicating with it by double doors, was the drawing-room. Here is the Drawing Room at Ditchley Park, Spelsbury, Oxon., a house rebuilt by James Gibbs (architect of the Radcliffe Camera, Oxford) after a fire in 1722.

139. The suite of state rooms in the great house included, on the same floor, a State Bedroom such as this one at Osterley Park, Middlesex, designed (including the splendid bed) by Robert Adam in 1775 for Robert Child the banker.

140. In the rational atmosphere of the 18th century, the library occupies the place of the private chapel of the middle ages. The Library at Easton Neston, Northants., built by Nicholas Hawksmoor in 1682 and later for Sir William Fermor. Later, such libraries usually had built-in bookcases.

141. When the great house was free of guests, the family used a small dining room, as here at Stourhead, Wiltshire. The room was often divided architecturally so as to provide a space at the end for service.

142. In the great houses of 1660 onwards, it was the height of fashion to have ceilings, especially over staircases, painted with classical scenes. At Melbury House, Melbury Sampford, Dorset, done soon after 1700 (probably by G. Lanscroon), this ceiling shows the council of the gods.

143. The framed staircase, originally a convenience, becomes a show-piece in itself. This staircase was inserted in Durham Castle by John Cosin, the Restoration bishop, who spent large sums on building. Staircases of the 18th century are still more magnificent.

144. The Georgian country house is to be found in Scotland, though much more rarely than in England. Invererne House, Morayshire, has basement service rooms; others have wings or pavilions for the same purpose.

145.
Gothic revival décor in the dining-room at Balnagowan Castle, Kildary, Ross.

146.

Wall-paper began to replace wall-painting and other types of hanging in the later 17th century, and was popular enough by 1712 for the Government to place a tax on it. The middle classes often had one or two rooms papered. Chinese wall-paper, as shown here in a house at Whitby, Yorkshire, was an expensive luxury; a design of birds and plants was the most popular, entirely hand-painted in imitation of the painted silk hangings found in rich Chinese homes. The general popularity of wall-paper had to wait until the tax was repealed in 1861.

147.

A bedchamber at Corehouse, Lanarkshire, with mainly 18th-century furniture, and a quite complete assemblage of toilet utensils: towels and towel rail, washstand with ewers and basins, soap dish; chamber pot and slop pail.

148.

Medieval builders are said to have used various devices to prevent the bricks at the back of a fireplace being burned away. The problem was solved first in Sussex and other centres of the iron industry in the 17th century by using a cast-iron fireback. When coal became more widely used, the fireback was even more necessary. This fireplace in the Old Cock Hotel, Halifax, has a fireback, what was called a range in the 17th century (i.e. a box to hold coal) and firedogs.

149. Cusworth Hall, West Yorkshire, has something like the medieval screens passage, but at the farther end of the hall from the entrance. The main stair is to one side and the kitchen to the other.

150.

In the 18th century, the middle-class house had stucco work somewhere—in the drawing-room, on the staircase, or in the best chamber. This house at Boston, Lincolnshire, built by a wine merchant, Henry Fydell, had deal panelling and a stucco ceiling in the hall; fifty years later the staircase walls were stuccoed in the then fashion, and a small part of the work can be seen over the drawing-room door.

151. In the great house from the 17th century onwards, the stables are usually two storey blocks, with chambers for grooms, etc. The stable court at Offchurch Bury, Warwickshire.

152. A servants' bedroom at Mamhead House, Devon, built in 1828 by Anthony Salvin: two maids to a bed, with a frame for curtains about the head and a shelf at the foot for clothes.

F

153.

The miller, whether his mill was driven by wind or water, had to live on the job and be prepared to get up in the night. This great brick-built water mill at Long Melford, Suffolk, has the mill house alongside.

154.

A new sight on the main roads was the toll-house put up by turnpike commissioners, such as this at Steanor Bottom Bar, Todmorden, West Yorkshire, designed so that the keeper could see all approaching traffic.

155. Another worker tied to his job was the lock-keeper on one of the new canals. Lock Cottage on the Shropshire Union Canal, Grindley Brook, Salop.

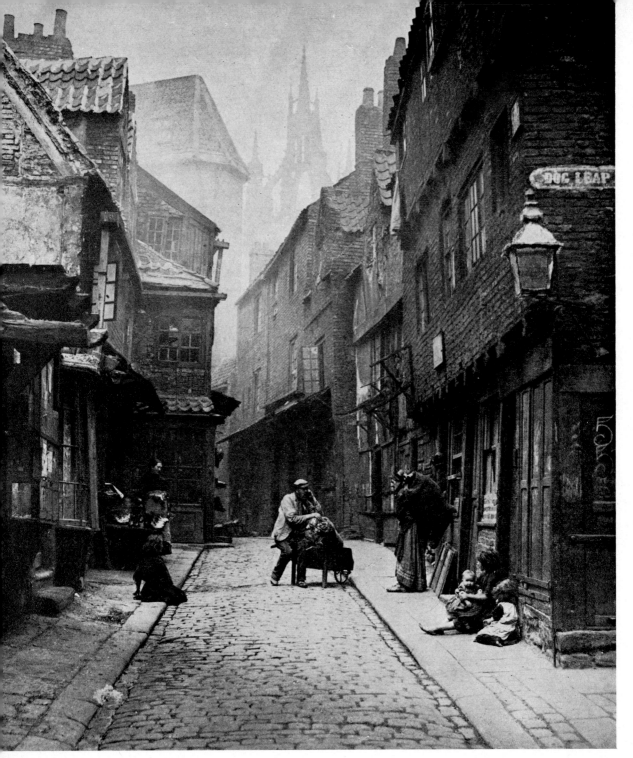

156. The medieval tradition of jettied building lasted long enough to be combined with the use of brick, as at Newcastle-upon-Tyne.

157. The early 18th-century shop, such as this in St. George's Square, Stamford, had a reticent, almost medieval, look; it was still a house with its front room designed for retail trade.

158. By the end of the 18th century, shop windows were made for displaying goods at all hours. The parlour over the shop is an essential aspect of the great growth of retail shop-keeping from the 17th century onwards, because by that period there was so much more traffic to sit and watch than there had been in the medieval town. Georgian bow windows added to a medieval shop (notice the jetty) in St. Mary's Street, Stamford.

159 & 160. The characteristic middle-class London house of 1660 onwards; three or four storeys with a basement kitchen looking on to an area, and (after about 1750) with a coal store under the pavement. ⟨159⟩ House in Walnut Tree Walk, Lambeth. ⟨160⟩ Coal hole cover in the pavement of Nevern Square, Earl's Court.

161. The terrace house most commonly has a narrow entrance hall leading to a staircase, with parlour in front and living-room behind. Scotch Street, Whitehaven, Cumberland.

162. The staircase in a terrace house, lighted only by a skylight; if the house was of reasonable size an open well allowed some light to reach the ground floor. Kensington Square, London.

163. The London design of terrace houses with basement kitchen, area and railings was adopted in Dublin, Edinburgh and fashionable provincial towns. Abbey Street, Bath.

164. Architects of middle-class terrace houses in Bath did their best to provide their clients with space to entertain; hence these double rooms in Brock Street.

165. 19th-century terrace houses in the north had cellars but no area, so that the cellars were very ill-lit, as here in Mount Street, Liverpool. They had to be barred to keep out intruders, and were used mainly as coal cellars.

166. The herring industry was flourishing and fishing ports everywhere grew in the 18th century. Here is a perspective of rows of cottages at Whitby, crowded under the hill on which the church stands.

167. With the rapid growth of population, the backs of the long, narrow properties in old towns were filled with cottages, and the consequent arrangement of closed courts with a tunnel entrance was also adopted for new development. The Hen and Chickens Yard, Newark, Nottinghamshire.

168. There are flats or tenements in the fishing port of Whitby, Yorkshire, because the constricted site round the harbour lent itself particularly to that form of building.

169.

In several regions the textile industry—silk and woollen weaving, stocking knitting—was based on the home from the late 17th century to the middle of the 19th. London silk weavers first took to using garrets for the purpose, and houses with top shops are characteristic of this type of industry. Early Victorian silk weavers' houses in London Road, Leek, Staffordshire.

170.

The establishment of cotton mills and other factories compelled industrialists to build houses for their workers. The dwellings put up by the Strutt family at Belper and Milford, Derbyshire, must have been model housing by contemporary standards. This row at Hopping Hill, Milford, provides living-room and kitchen, two bedrooms above (both with a fireplace) and a large garret. There are many ingenious features, such as cast-iron casement windows (mostly removed in this pair), adjustable gutter brackets and cast-iron door numbers. There is a small garden at the front and a yard at the back.

171. Scottish weavers, left to themselves, continued to build single-storey cottages, such as this at Kilbarchan, Renfrewshire; advantage might be taken of a sloping site to make a room over the weaving shop. This house is now a local museum and weaving centre.

173.
In Scottish villages and small towns, two-storey houses with a forestair on the street are common. It may be the result of dividing a large house into two flats or tenements, but in this instance, in Shore Gate, Crail, Fifeshire, the site slopes and so the idea of the medieval first-floor house, with storage space below, naturally persists.

172. When the factory system reached the Scottish textile industry, employers sometimes put up tenements for their workers, such as this range at Blantyre, Lanarkshire, or the blocks erected at New Lanark by David Dale. They naturally adopted the external stair turret of Edinburgh tenements. David Livingstone was born here.

174. When the new planned towns and villages of Scotland were developed in the 18th century, storeyed building was nearly always enforced—two-storey houses in the villages, and tenements in the towns, as here at Inverary. They give such places a truly urban character, and in this instance match the scale of the church.

75. The few entirely new country houses of the Victorian age are full-blooded exercises in revivalism, either Gothic, Tudor or Jacobean. This is Harlaxton Manor, Lincolnshire, built mainly by Anthony Salvin in 1831 onwards. A contemporary called it 'chaste and elegant', and a modern architectural historian has called it 'an easy and manageable style', but scarcely any houses of this scale and age are still in use as private houses. They were built when the incomes of the landed gentry were at their maximum, and domestic servants at their most plentiful; in present conditions they are unmanageable as homes.

76. Summerhouses were not unknown in the middle ages, and examples survive from every century since the 16th. This is one in Victorian Tudor style, by Gilbert Scott, in the grounds of Kelham Hall, Nottinghamshire, a great Victorian Gothic mansion.

177. Crawford Priory, Fifeshire, Scotland, is another testimonial to the scholarship of Victorian architects: this time in Gothic. Notice the great open hall, and the octagonal tower derived from the monastic chapter house.

178.

The hall of Goodrich Court, Herefordshire, built in 1828–31 for Sir Samuel Rush-Meyrick, a wealthy collector of medieval armour, to provide for him and his collection a suitable home. Notice the medieval roof and the Tudor fireplace, both scholarly imitations of the real thing.

179. In country houses of the Scottish Highlands, interest now centred mainly on hunting. The crofters had been turned out of their holdings in favour of deer. The Trophy Room at Balnagowan Castle, Kildary, Ross-shire.

180.

The Victorian conservatory stands mid-way in line of descent between the Georgian orangery, often a fine piece of architecture in its own right, and the tiny greenhouse in a suburban back garden, mass-produced and sold through mass advertising. The Victorian conservatory was entered from the drawing-room, bringing tropical plants into the house; now many of them are, like this one, neglected and used at most as sun-lounges.

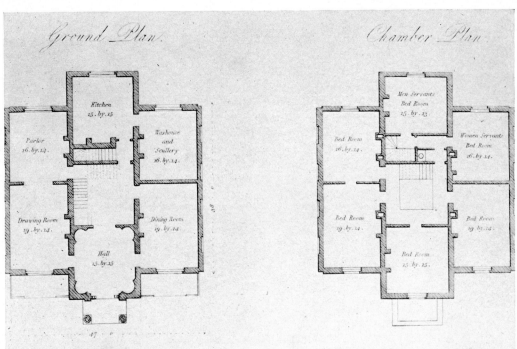

181 & 182. From the early years of the 18th century, the design of houses was increasingly influenced by books about architecture—first the great houses, then villas for men of more modest means, and eventually the cottages of farm labourers. This view and plan of a country villa come from a pattern book published in 1808: C. A. Busby's *Designs for Villas and Country Houses* (*Adapted with economy to the Comforts and Elegances of Country Life*).

183. The idea of semi-detached houses (together with that of flats) was evolved for the smallest houses and adapted, under the pressure of space and site values in town development, for larger houses. This pair of semi-detached villas in the Gothic style, at Ninetree Hill, Bristol, might have come from one of the architects' pattern books of the early 19th century.

184. Oxford preserved as long as any place the tradition of the basement kitchen, because that design suited the social habits of a university city, and the speculative builders responsible were able to combine reasonable density with some pretension. The houses are narrow in proportion to size, with only two principal rooms to a floor, and the roof space is fully utilized.

185 & 186.

The tradition of the Georgian spas persisted in Bristol and in Clifton, on the western outskirts. The basement kitchen was now at ground level and so better lit, both in the terraces (Egerton Terrace, City Road, Bristol ⟨185⟩) and in the spacious semi-detached houses (Tyndall's Park Road, Clifton ⟨186⟩).

187.

Sea-bathing began to bring visitors to places like Lyme Regis in the 18th century. Lyme has retained the aspect of a village because it did not offer sufficient scope for the large-scale development which transformed Brighton or ▸ Hove (*The Town* ⟨148⟩).

188. A Jacobean interior, perfectly Victorianised. This house in Oxford was built about 1628 (the date of the plaster ceiling) and served later as the palace of bishops of Oxford. This room on the first floor was Bishop King's drawing-room. Every item of furniture and decoration is impeccably of its period and nothing characteristic is missing. The Old Palace, St. Aldate's.

189.

In modern times the aisled hall of Tiptoft's Manor, Wimbish, Essex, became the kitchen. Notice the bell board fixed to the 14th-century moulded timber pier. Such a bell system, operated by an elaboration of wires, pulleys and cranks buried in walls, could summon servants to any of the principal rooms, both upstairs and down.

190. A Victorian lower-middle class family at tea.

191 & 192. Two homes on the eve of the First World War. One a superior working class home; notice the boys' Eton collars. The other a poor home in the East End of London, with empty plates and tins.

193. The kitchen at Hayes Barton, East Budleigh, Devon (the birthplace of Sir Walter Ralegh). West Country folk have been reluctant to give up the hearth fire: hence this 19th-century iron range with an oven underneath the fire. Notice also the fire window on the left, and the arched opening of a bread oven on the right. Hobs have been built up in brick, flanking the fire. The visible items of furniture complete the picture of a kitchen of fifty years ago.

194. A working-class bedroom of about 1910: notice the brass bedstead and marble-topped washstand; the framed texts, family groups and sentimental prints on the walls, and the mass of ill-designed china ornaments on the dressing-table.

195.

The great cheese press in the dairy at New Hall, Chirk, Denbighshire.

196.

A cool storage place in a suburban villa of about 1830. The floor is sunk three feet below ground, and there is a stone shelf round the walls. No modern house needs such a larder, because shops are so accessible that housekeeping on a large and careful scale is unnecessary, and because hire purchase has brought the refrigerator within the reach of many households.

197. This house at East Kilbride, Lanarkshire, a developed form of the house shown in ⟨130⟩, is typical of the houses of small lairds, farmers and ministers in Scotland from about 1775 onwards. A description of the manse at Kildonan, Sutherland, given by Donald Sage fits it perfectly: downstairs a parlour, a bedroom and an intervening closet; in the 'upper flat', as he called it, a dining-room, another bedroom and closet and two garrets in the roof. One wing contained the nursery, the kitchen and the byre: the other, barn and stable.

198. A non-parlour type of cottage was built by smallholders in the Lincolnshire Fens in the 19th century. The one entrance led into a scullery, with a living-room beyond. A ladder led to two small bedrooms with windows in the gable ends. Cottage at Stickney, Lincolnshire.

199.

This cottage at Jurby, Isle of Man, its sod walls a home for giant convolvulus, was photographed in 1897. Smoke can be seen rising from a wattle chimney over the gable-end hearth; no glazed windows are visible. Whatever the age of the cottage, it shows the persistence of an ancient mode of life to the end of the 19th century.

200.

The interior of a Welsh *croglofft* cottage, showing the entrance to the loft, reached by a ladder, or simply by climbing on to the back of a chair. Ffynnon Goy Isaf, Llanychaer, Pembrokeshire.

201, 202 & 203.

From the end of the 18th century improving landlords began to pay attention to the housing of workers on their estates, and a characteristic type of village emerged, with very often an attempt at the picturesque, especially in houses built near the great house itself: ⟨201⟩ the gardener's cottage at Somerleyton Hall, Suffolk; ⟨202⟩ a row of semi-detached cottages on the Russell estate at Ampthill, Bedfordshire, dated 1816. ⟨203⟩ The architect of these cottages built for farm labourers at Sudbury, Derbyshire by Lord Vernon, was awarded a medal by the Society of Arts for the design. Each cottage has a porch, living-room, scullery, pantry, fuel store, piggery 'and other conveniences, with cess-pit and ash-pit. Upstairs are the parents' bedroom, and the male and female bedrooms. The scullery has a washing copper, a sink and a fireclay baking-oven. Each cottage has a well, besides which the rainwater from the roofs is conveyed to tanks for domestic use. There is a pump fixed over the sink in the scullery. The walls are constructed in two thicknesses, with a hollow between, to prevent damp.'

204. Kiln Yard, Whitby, Yorkshire. Such yards were a children's playground and a drying ground for washing. Notice the wash-tub with a dolly in it.

205. In Milford, Derbyshire, rows of back-to-back houses strung along the slope of the valley have a roadway on the upper side; houses on the lower side are reached by a footpath. Coal is dumped from road level down this chute, and the householder then carries it to the store under the stairs.

206. Floors of cobbles or pitched stone were still being laid in the 19th century where suitable material was plentiful and any alternative more expensive. At Llanidloes, Montgomeryshire, these attractive pavements can be matched by patterned floors inside houses, and by pitching to mark graves in the churchyard.

207. There is a gloomy contrast between these Llanidloes houses, which still preserve some elements of a folk culture, and houses in the back streets of Victorian Nottingham, built by speculators to let to factory workers. They are a cut-down version of the ingenious but spacious terrace housing of Georgian London. The front door leads straight into the parlour—notice the flowers in its window. There is a coal cellar under the parlour, and the foot-scraper serves as a reminder of the condition of town streets in 1890.

208. Though the houses in ⟨207⟩ may present a seemly front, backyards, originally having no more than a small scullery and out-door lavatory, easily turned into a crowded squalor of washing lines, sheds and the like. These rows are in Stepney, London.

209. In some places rows were built with no through access or ventilation—'not throughs', as Seebohm Rowntree called them in his investigation of poverty in York. This row at Newark, Nottinghamshire, presents a completely blank wall on the farther side. Each house has living-room, scullery and two bedrooms, and, unlike the Leeds back-to-backs, a strip of garden.

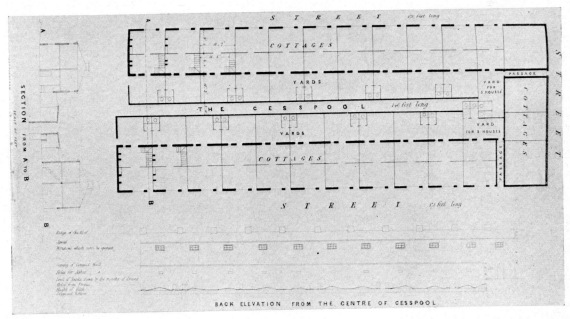

210 & 211. Houses at Preston, Lancashire, built before 1844 for workers in the cotton mills in the background. They were condemned at that time by a Royal Commission, because of their sanitary arrangements: sewage from earth closets in each enclosed yard (some containing pigsties) flowed in the open sewer between the rows to a cesspool which belonged to the landlord, who emptied it and sold the contents twice a year. Apart from such remediable defects, these illustrations show how the Industrial Revolution planted houses of urban type in the midst of the countryside.

H

212 & 213.
The earliest blocks of flats in England were model working-class dwellings. ⟨212⟩ Those in Gunthorpe Street, Commercial Road, Stepney, have verandas, or streets in the air, and the one whitewashed flat indicates the size of a dwelling. The blocks in St. Pancras ⟨213⟩ have roads railed off, making 'a capital play-ground for children'; very similar blocks were erected in Birkenhead for dock workers.

214. In some northern towns, back-to-back housing continued well into this century, and made a major contribution to the growth of cities such as Leeds: so much so that they are being reconditioned rather than replaced. These have a cellar, a living-room and scullery, two bedrooms over and a large attic.

215. Once working-class houses were linked with water mains and sewers, the earth closet away from the house—at the bottom of the yard, or in the centre of the court—gave way to water closets such as this, usually entered from outside the house.

216. The kitchen in a Leeds house of about 1900, with a large stoneware sink, glazed yellow; a cold water tap above it, and the washing copper alongside. The double gas-ring for cooking is a later improvement. These houses are now being very skilfully modernised.

217. Still another variant on the back-to-back, suitable for a narrow West Riding valley. These four-storey rows have one row of two-storey houses on top of another, the upper row entered from a road at third-floor level. Little Knowl Terrace, Todmorden, was built in 1861.

218. In Newcastle-upon-Tyne, the problem was solved by building terraced flats. Only the paired doorways indicate that these are not ordinary terrace houses. One doorway leads to the ground-floor flat, the next to the one upstairs.

219. The discovery that paraffin oil could be got from bituminous shale created the Scottish mining village of Broxburn, West Lothian. Some rows consist of single-roomed cottages, others two-roomed; none have gardens or even back-yards, though allotments are available. There is one detached wash-house to four houses. These two-roomed cottages have a large porch on the street, which had a water closet from the beginning and is now also adapted for cooking. Each of the two rooms has a pair of box recesses on one wall, curtained off during the daytime. The farther room was the parlour.

220. Whisky distillers in Edinburgh built 'colonies' of model housing for their workers in the middle of the 19th century, in this Scottish version of terraced flats. Each row has upstairs flats entered from one side of the row and downstairs flats entered from the other. This is a row off Glenogle Road, Edinburgh.

221. Time and again the reports of Victorian (and later) social reformers commented on the inadequacy of sanitary provisions in large cities. 'One toilet to eight families' is illustrated here in the Gorbals area of Glasgow.

222.

In the Scottish lowlands, cottages were rebuilt in stone in the 19th century without any change in the way of life of the farm workers living in them. The major improvement was a piped water supply, brought to stand pipes on the kerb. Dewarton, Midlothian.

223.

Rothes is one of the planned villages of Morayshire, begun in 1766. Many of the original houses were single storey, but New Street is Victorian, with characteristically Scottish dormers, taken by an architect from the baronial tradition and incorporated in these simple houses.

224.

The attic bay window is, to an English observer, the most startling development of the Scottish cottage tradition. Here in the fishing villages of north-east Scotland, such as Seatown, Macduff, the loft was used mainly for fishing gear, as it was in 17th-century Yarmouth. Since about 1900, the use of bright paints has spread from fishing boats to cottages; remarkably vivid combinations are to be seen, and joints are picked out in stone walling or painted on to cement rendering.

225. Highland black houses on the island of South Uist in the Outer Hebrides, still inhabited when this photograph was taken (1934). They had thick walls of turf or stone with the thatched roof resting on an inner edge of the walls.

226. The old and the new side by side against a rocky hillside on the island of Barra. The old house, with its gable-end fireplace, is probably now used as a cow byre. The new house, with its one and a half storeys and lofty dormers ('storm windows' in Scotland), is thoroughly in the Scottish tradition.

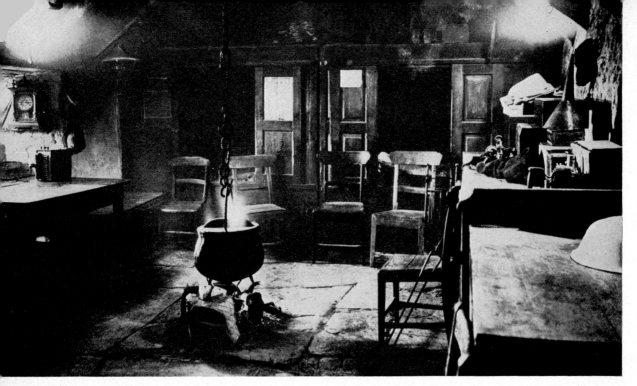

227. The older type of black house had a central hearth, as in this Orkney example; the smoke found its way out as it could. This is, for Orkney, a very superior home, because it has a couple of box beds at the end, and is well furnished.

228. In most parts of the Highlands, the central hearth was superseded in the 19th century by a gable-end fireplace, over it a wide timber hood. The interior of a Shetland house about half a century ago.

229. In recent times the Scottish box bed became a mere recess, curtained off from the rest of one room in which many working-class families live. When in 1961 the Queen visited this district of Glasgow, the Gorbals, she was reported as wondering how a family could manage in a 'single end' like this.

230. A Welsh country home in recent times, the dresser crowded with plates and china ornaments, the table covered with oil-cloth under a cloth laid diamond-wise for a cup of tea; wall-paper, wall clock, heavily cut glass sugar bowl—all the details, although the photograph was taken in the Treweryn Valley in 1957, might well be thirty years earlier.

231. One of the special consequences of the English tradition of one house, one family, is that many old houses have been subdivided, usually after the neighbourhood has come down in the world. Here is a fine stone house in Sladden Street, Boothtown, Halifax, originally built by a successful yeoman clothier, now three cottages. The hall of the old house is one cottage, each of the wings another. The number of television aerials is one of the clearest indications of this process.

232.
A large medieval fireplace will take a modern cooker: Faenol Fawr, Bodelwyddan, Flintshire.

233. The garden city movement restored ideas of space and dignity to town life, even if its standards of density and architecture were inappropriate to cities (see *The Town* ⟨78⟩). Welwyn Garden City, illustrated here, was established in 1920, following Letchworth, which was established by Ebenezer Howard in 1903.

234. The greatest single landmark in the history of the English house is the Housing Act of 1919, passed to enable local authorities to build the cheap houses to rent, which private enterprise, in the twenty-five years before 1914, had shown itself incapable of providing. The best council housing showed the influence of the garden city concept, though densities were very much greater, and a 'cottagey' style of building prevailed. Here, at Nottingham, is a design harking back to the medieval or Tudor house, but actually three dwellings.

235. In Scotland, native tradition persists in the flatted villa. This is a group of four in Corstorphine, Edinburgh, built since 1945, mullioned windows and all. The right-hand door leads to the upstairs flat, the next to the one below it.

236. Private enterprise in the 1930s ran riot with detached and semi-detached villas with Tudor gables and bay windows. Here are all the hall-marks of 20th-century suburban life: concrete street lamps, markers in the hedge for water mains, cherry trees planted by the local authority; the latticed gate hiding the concrete drive to the garage, stained glass in the hall door and—the most recent status symbol—the television aerial for *both* B.B.C. and I.T.V.

237.
The 'cloakroom' which is to be found in middle-class houses, with a wash-basin and a water closet in it, is really the successor of the medieval basin, ewer and sink for use after meals ⟨18,19⟩, but the bathroom is entirely modern. As visitors to great houses will have noticed, Georgian houses had no bathroom. It began to appear in luxurious houses about 1880, and became a standard part of houses of all classes only in the period 1918 to 1939.

238. The English town-dweller has accepted much less readily than the Scottish, or the French, the idea of making his home on one floor of a multi-storey block. Now, if he is fortunate, the Londoner can look out on an English park. The L.C.C.'s Alton Estate, Wandsworth.

239. Modern local authority housing in Scotland has appropriate traditions to use. These are single-storey dwellings for old people and blocks of flats at Dumfries.

Index

The figures in italics refer to illustrations on p. 77 onwards

ABERGELE, Denbighshire, *63, 94*

Adam, Robert, 50, *136, 139*

Addington, Great, Northamptonshire, *77*

Affleck Castle, Angus, *29*

Airth, Stirling, 53

Airton, West Yorkshire, *99*

Aisled hall, 16, 21, 41, *11*

Almshouses, 32, 40, *85*

American cloth, 61

Ampthill, Bedfordshire, *202*

Architects, 50, 59, 62, *203, 223*

'Area', 59, *159–60, 163*

Aslockton, Nottinghamshire, *112*

Audley End, Essex, 34

Aynho, Northamptonshire, *79*

BACK boiler, 67

Back-to-back housing, 61–2, *205, 214*

Back-to-earth housing, 62

Baking, 41, 54, *25, 111, 203*

Banker, 21

Bannockburn, Stirling, 64

Barbon, Nicholas, 56, 59

Barns, 32

Barrington Court, Somerset, *33*

Barrowby, Lincolnshire, *84*

Basement
See Cellar

Basement, vaulted, 71, *1, 2, 76*

Basement services, 35, 57–60, *38, 71–2, 144, 159, 163, 184–6*

Bastels, 28

Bath, 56, *163–4*

Bathrooms, 66, 67, *237*

Battlements, 38, 39

Bay window, *16, 80–1, 224*

Bayeux Tapestry, *1, 4*

Bed, 21, 22, 70

Bedrooms, *125–7, 139, 194*
See also Sleeping room

Bell board, *189*

Belper, Derbyshire, 62

Bench, 21, 22

Billiards, 35, *48*

Birmingham, 70

Black house, *225, 227*

Black Notley, Essex, *50*

Blantyre, Lanarkshire, *172*

Bledington, Gloucestershire, *127*

Blenheim Palace, Oxfordshire, 47, 48, *135*

Bletchingdon, Oxfordshire, 63

Bodelwyddan, Flintshire, *232*

Bonshaw Tower, Dumfriesshire, *125*

Borthwick Castle, Midlothian, *31*

Bosham, Sussex, *1*

Boston, Lincolnshire, *150*

Bower, 25

Bowls, indoor, *48*

Box beds, 46, 51, 52, 55, 61, 64, *219, 227, 229*

Brackley, Northamptonshire, *85*

Bradford, Yorkshire, *98, 100*

Brant Broughton, Lincolnshire, 43

Brantingby, Leicestershire, 65

Brewing, 41, 55, *25*

Brick building, 32–3, 46, *3, 37, 44, 46, 66, 124, 134, 156*

Bristol, 56, *183, 185–6*

Britannia Illustrata (Kyp), 48

Broxburn, West Lothian, 63, *219*

Buckley, Flintshire, *116*

Budleigh, East, Devon, *193*

Building industry, 70

Bulcote, Nottinghamshire, *87*

Bungalow, 17, 60, *239*

Burford, Oxfordshire, *2*

Burnsall, West Yorkshire, *104*

Burton Agnes, East Yorkshire, *47*

Busby, C. A., *181–2*

'But and ben', 53

Buttery, 23, 24, 41, 46, *30*

Byre, 26, 27, *88*

CALSTOCK, Cornwall, *42*

Carpets, 45, 46, 66

Cast iron, use of, *170*

Castle Howard, North Yorkshire, 47, 48, *49*

Castles, 27–8

Cavity walls, *203*

Cawdor Castle, Nairnshire, *74*

Cecil, Robert, Earl of Salisbury, *41*

Cefn, Denbighshire, *19*

Ceilings, 38, 50, *49, 52, 53, 59, 92–3, 143, 188*

Cellar, 18, 23, 24, 30, 57, 65, *165, 207, 214*
vaulted, *1–3*

Cerrig-y-Drudion, Denbighshire, *62, 96*

Cesspool, *210–11*

Chagford, Devon, 27

Chair, 21, 38, *10*

Chamber, 21, 23, 25, 28, 31, 34, 36, 39, 40, 42, 50, *5, 28–32, 49, 50, 53, 58, 94, 103*
smoking, 42
See also Solar

Chamber pot, 31, 44, *147*

Chapel, 49, *3, 29, 140*

Cheese press, *195*

Chester, 30

Chiddingfold, Kent, *80*

Chignall, Essex, *51*

Child, Robert, *139*

Chimney stack, *51, 66–70*
axial, 37, 42, 44, 60, *51, 83, 112*
backing on passage, 27, 46, *78, 88–9, 94, 122*
gable end, 51, 52, 53, *111, 115, 117–18, 128, 130, 228*
lateral, 18, 37, *95–6, 123*
repair of, 60

Chirk, Denbighshire, *73, 195*

Chorley, Cheshire, *48*

Claypotts Castle, Angus, *40*

Cloakroom, *237*

Close stool, 44

Closet, 53, *128–9*
earth, 63, *112, 210–11*
tub, 58
water, 55, 59, 66, 67, *208, 215, 219, 221*

Coal chute, *205*
store, 57, 58, 59, 62, *160*

Cockburn, John, 54

Coker, West, Somerset, *12*

Coleshill, Berkshire, 47

Conservatory, 55, *180*

Copper, washing, 54, *203*
Corbridge, Northumberland, 28
Corehouse, Lanarkshire, *147*
Cosin, John, Bishop of Durham, *142*
Coster, 21
Cottingham, East Yorkshire, *129*
Cotton, Suffolk, *26*
Cotton Hall, Denbighshire, *73, 123*
Courtyard, 36, 37, 44, 48, *22–3, 74–5, 135*
  See also Yard
Cowhouse
  See Byre
Crail, Fifeshire, *173*
Cranborne, Dorset, *41*
Crawford, Fifeshire, *177*
Cream oven, *120*
Croglofft
  See Loft
Crosthwaite, Westmorland, *106*
Cruck construction, 16–17, 18, *44, 118*
Crundale, Kent, *70*
Cupar, Fifeshire, *36*
Cupboard, 22
  bed
  See Box bed
Cusworth, West Yorkshire, *149*

DAIRY, 27, 51, *30, 195*
Dais, 24
Dale, David, 68–9
Dartington, Devon, 33, *23*
Date stones, *60–1, 64, 67, 99, 118, 123, 130*
Deal, Kent, *134*
Dewarton, Midlothian, *222*
Dining room, 35, 40, 44, 49, 57, 58, 60, 68, *52, 141, 145*
Dock workers, *213*
Dog-gate, *105*
Dolly, *204*
Dormer window, 36, 40, 44, *75, 113–14, 126–7, 223, 226*
Dosser, 21
'Double pile', 43, 51, *87*
Double terrace, *217*
Dovecotes, 33, *79*
Down St. Mary, Devon, *43, 120*
Drain
  See Sink
Draughts, 70, *53*
Drawing room, 35, 49, 50, 57, 59, 60, 68, *133, 138*
Dresser, 51, *230*
Dressing room, 49, 59

Dumfries, *239*
Durham, *142*
Dyffryn, Claerwen, Radnorshire, *118*

EASTBURY Park, Dorset, 48
Eating room
  See Dining room
Eaton Constantine, Salop, *83*
Eddington, Kent, *126*
Edinburgh, 60, 61, 65, *59, 109, 220, 235*
Egerton, Kent, *5*
Electricity, 56
Elie, Fifeshire, *76*
Enclosure of open fields, 50, 51, 55, *132*
Engels, F., 71
Entry
  See Passage
Exminster, Devon, *25*

FALKLAND, Fifeshire, *130*
Family, types of, 14–15
Fermor, Sir William, *140*
Fire window, *90, 193*
Fireplace, 36, 43, 46, 51, 53, 54, *9, 10, 31, 37, 78, 89, 90, 101–3, 117, 122, 128–30, 148, 228, 232*
  See also Chimney stack
Firescreen, 22
First floor hall, 18, 28–9, 38, 39, 53, 59, *1, 3, 76, 173*
Fishponds, *26*
Flats, 61, 65, 66, 70, 71, *212–13, 238*
Flatted villas, *235*
Floorcloth, 66
Flooring, 38, 50, *13, 43, 107, 136, 206*
Forestair
  See Staircase
Forncett St. Mary's, Norfolk, *13*
Frescoes, 58
Fulbeck, Lincolnshire, *121*
Furniture, 19, 38–9, 43, 46–7, 52, 54, 55–6, 61, 69, *14, 48, 53, 72, 92–3, 107, 119, 139, 147, 188, 194, 227, 230*
Fydell, Henry, *150*
Fyvie Castle, Aberdeenshire, *39*

GABLES, 45, 52, *40, 109, 114, 134*
Gainsborough, Lincolnshire, *37*
Gallery, 30, 34, 44, *22, 48, 100, 106*
Garage, 17, 61, *236*

Gardens, 63, 64, *170, 209, 219, 233–4*
Garderobe, 31, 44, *20, 21, 23, 28, 37*
Garrets, 35, *45, 71, 73, 126–7*
  See also Vance roof
Gas, 66–7, *216*
Gibb, James, *138*
Glapton, Nottinghamshire, 90–1
Glasgow, 60, *221, 229*
Glastonbury, Somerset, *24*
Glazing, 20–1, 28, 45, 61, *15, 62–5*
Goodrich, Herefordshire, *178*
Gothic revival, 145, *175–7, 183*
Grindley Brook, Salop, *155*
Gunports, 39, *40*

HADDON Hall, Derbyshire, *22*
Halifax, 70, *101, 148, 231*
Hall, 18–19, 20, 23, 24, 34, 35, 37, 40, 41, 47, 49, 50, 61, 69, *5–7, 11, 28–9, 31–2, 41, 50, 100, 107, 119, 121, 136, 161, 177–8*
  See also First floor hall
Hardware, 62, 67
Hardwick Hall, Derbyshire, *33, 34*
Harlaxton, Lincolnshire, *175*
Harrington, Sir John, 67
Harrison, William, 70
Hawksmoor, Nicholas, *140*
Hearth, central, 19, 52, *6, 8, 11, 12, 227*
  fire, *89, 92, 193*
Hendre, Flintshire, *68*
Hengrave Hall, Suffolk, 35
Hervey, Frederick, Bishop of Derry, 49
Higher Grenofen, Whitchurch, Devon, 27
Highland zone, 26, 28, 29
Hire purchase, 68
Holbeach, Lincolnshire, *115*
Honington, Salop, *117*
Houghton, Norfolk, 49, *137*
Housing legislation, 65, *234*
  societies, 65–6
Howard, Ebenezer, *233*
Hunting lodge, *41*

ICKWORTH, Suffolk, 49
Industrial Revolution, 51, 62, 64, 66, *210–11*
Industry, domestic, 42, 44–5
  fishing, 46, 54, *166, 168, 224*
  mining, 63, *219*
  textile, *169–72, 210–11*
'Ingle neuk', *95*
Inventories, 19
Inveraray, Argyllshire, *174*
Invererne, Morayshire, *144*
Isleworth, Middlesex, *136*

JAMESTONE, Pembrokeshire, 95

Jetty, 5, 16, 45, 46, 110, 156, 158

Jones, Inigo, 47, 56

Jug and basin, 31, 18

Jurby, Isle of Man, 199

KAIL yard, 54

Kelham, Nottinghamshire, 176

Kellie Castle, Fifeshire, 75

Kendal, Westmorland, 105

Kennet Village, Clackmannan, 63

Kentangaval, Barra, 226

Kilbarchan, Renfrewshire, 171

Kilbride, East, Lanarkshire, 197

Kildary, Ross-shire, 145, 179

King's Lynn, Norfolk, 46, 108

Kingston, Herefordshire, 35

Kirby Hall, Northamptonshire, 34

Kitchen, 23, 24, 35, 41, 44, 46, 49–50, 52, 57, 58, 60, 68, 13, 24–5, 31, 40

LACOCK, Wiltshire, 44

Ladder, 37, 198, 200

Lake District, 25

Lanark, New, 63, 68–9

Landlords, 51, 54, 56, 62, 65, 201–3, 210–11

Lanscroon, G., 143

Larder, 196

Lavenham, Suffolk, 17

Layer Marney, Essex, 34

Leeds, 70, 214–16

Leek, Staffordshire, 169

Leverington, Cambridgeshire, 66

Library, 49, 58, 140

Lincoln, 20

Linoleum, 66

Liverpool, 14, 65, 165

Llanbeulan, Anglesey, 61

Llandegla, Denbighshire, 52

Llanerfyl, Montgomeryshire, 124

Llangynog, Montgomeryshire, 91

Llanidloes, Montgomeryshire, 206

Llanychaer, Pembrokeshire, 200

Local authority housing, 70, 234

Lock-keeper, 155

Lodgings, 22, 23, 32, 37

Loft, 51, 52, 54, 200

London, 44–5, 56–9, 65, 69–70, 110, 159–60, 162, 208, 212–13, 238

Long house, 17, 26, 27, 28, 51, 52, 88–9, 118

Longleat, Wiltshire., 33

Longthorpe, Northamptonshire, 21

Louvre, 24, 12

Luddesdown Court, Kent, 9

Luton, Bedfordshire, 55

Lyme Regis, Dorset, 187

Lyth, Westmorland, 119

MACDUFF, Fifeshire, 224

Madeley, Staffordshire, 46

Maenan, Caernarvonshire, 54

Maisonettes, 71

Mamhead, Devon, 152

Manchester, 71

Marcham, Berkshire, 37

Market Deeping, Lincolnshire, 18

Marlborough, Duke of, 135

Martock, Somerset, 8

Melbury Sampford, Dorset, 143

Melford, Long, Suffolk, 153

Mereworth, Kent, 49

Milford, Derbyshire, 62, 170, 205

Miller, 153

Moat, 26

Monastery, medieval, 17, 18, 32

Monk's Eleigh, Suffolk, 7, 67

Morley, Derbyshire, 18

Morning room, 68

NAYLAND, Suffolk, 14

Necessary house, 31

Nelson, Lancashire, 131

Newark, Nottinghamshire, 167, 209

Newcastle upon Tyne, 65, 70, 156, 218

Norman Conquest, 15, 18, 1

Northiam, Sussex, 6

Northop, Flintshire, 103

Northumberland, Duke of, 136

'Not through' housing, 61, 209

Nottingham, 30, 58, 207, 234

Nursery, 68

OFFCHURCH, Warwickshire, 133

Oil lamp, 66

Oilcloth, 66

'Open plan', 69

Oriel, 32
  See also Bay window

Orkneys, 15, 227

Osterley, Middlesex, 139

Otley, Suffolk, 34

Oven, 193
  See also Baking

Owen, Robert, 63

Oxford, 60, 184, 188

PAINTED cloths, 21, 38, 55
  plaster, 21, 38, 31, 56–9
  walls, 224

Palladio, 48, 59

Pant Glas Uchaf, Caernarvonshire, 92–3

Pantiles, 8, 113

Pantry, 24

Pargeting, 32, 82

Parham, Suffolk, 16

Paris, 70

Parlour, 23, 25, 27, 37, 40, 42, 50, 52, 57, 58, 66, 69, 43, 52, 70, 102, 121, 158, 207

Parsonage house, 18, 133

Partitions, 43, 51, 43, 107

Passage, 19, 23, 31, 37, 41, 43, 52, 8, 13, 30, 78, 88–9, 94, 149
  underground, 48

Pattern books, 50, 56, 129, 133, 181–2

Pawnbroker, 68

Pele tower
  See Tower house

Penrhos, Monmouthshire, 43

Petherton, South, Devon, 78

Pewter, 39, 46

Pigs, 64

Piscina, 18

Plaster ornament, 47, 53, 54, 82, 101, 150, 188

Platform houses, 28

Pope, Alexander, 47–8

Population, growth of, 32, 167

Porch, 50, 27, 33, 46, 77, 99, 203

Portraits, 40

Pratt, Sir Roger, 47, 87

Preston, Lancashire, 64, 210–11

Preston Court, Gloucestershire, 45

Preston Patrick Hall, Westmorland, 15

Privy, 44, 62, 64–5
  See also Closet

RANGE, 102–3, 119, 148

Rasmussen, S. E., 69, 70

Raynham Hall, Norfolk, 47, 71

Rectory
  See Parsonage house

Renaissance, 20, 33, 48, 59, 110

Reredorter, 31

Roof, types of, 16, 18, 19, 23, 26, 43, 4, 6–8, 50–1, 54, 87, 98, 114, 122, 178

Rothes, Morayshire, *223*
Rowarth, Derbyshire, *60*
Rugs, snip, 67
Rush-Meyrick, Sir Samuel, *178*

St. Albans, Earl of, 56, 58
Saloon, 47, 49, *137*
Salvin, Anthony, *152*
Sanitation, 58
Schools, 32, *104*
Scott, George Gilbert, *176*
Scraper, *207*
Screen, 19, 51–2, 60, *47*, *111*
Screveton, Nottinghamshire, *10*
Scullery, 58, *198*, *208*
Second-hand dealer, 68
Semi-detached housing, 60, 61, *115*, *183–4*, *186*, *202*
Servants, 34, 35, 37, 40, 51, 54, 59, 68, *32*, *71–3*, *108*, *119*, *126–7*, *151–2*, *175*, *189*
See also Lodgings
Service room, 23, 26, *41*
Seton, Sir Alexander, *39*
Settle, 21
Sewer, 64
Sheffield, 64
Shetland, *228*
Shingles, wooden, *4*
Shippen
See Byre
Shop window, 17, *157–8*
Shuffleboard, *48*
Sibton, Suffolk, *82*
Sinclair, Sir John, 55
'Single end', 63, *229*
Sink, 31, 64, *18*, *19*, *216*
Sitting room, 26, *41*
Sleeping room, 47, 51, 62, 69, 70
Slop stone
See Sink
Smythson, Robert, 33, 47, *38*
Solar, 23, 24, *8*, *14*, *16*
Somerleyton, Norfolk, *201*
Speculative builder, 62, *236*
Spelsbury, Oxfordshire, *138*
'Spence', 52
Stables, 32, *151*
Staircase, 45, 49, 50, 53, 56–7, 60, 69, *28*, *86*, *131*, *161–2*
    forestair, 30, 46, 65, *173*
    framed, 35, *35–6*, *74*, *142*
    newel, 35, 37, 44, *32*, *33*, *75*, *92*
    outside, 23, *1*
    turret, 43, 64, *29*, *32*, *33*, *35*, *40*, *76*, *108–9*, *172*

Stamford, Lincolnshire, *57*, *81*, *157–8*
Stand pipe, *222*
Steeple Aston, Oxfordshire, *128*
Stickney, Lincolnshire, *69*, *198*
Stone building, 30
Stonesby, Leicestershire, *113*
Storeyed house, 17–18, 23, 24, 29, 36, 40, 44, 51–2, 53, 54, *5*, *33*, *77*, *86*, *110*, *151*, *173–4*
See also Tenements
Stourton, Wiltshire, *141*
Stow, West, Suffolk, *56*
Stow on the Wold, Gloucestershire, *64*
Stratford-on-Avon, Warwickshire, *25*
'Streets in the air', 65, *212*
Strickland Roger, Westmorland, *30*
Strutt family, 62, *170*
Stucco, 58
Study, 68
Sudbury, Derbyshire, 203
Summer house, *176*
Sunk house, 17
Sutton Bonington, Nottinghamshire, *86*
Symmetry in design, 33, 53, *33*, *77*, *84*, *121–3*, *130*

Table, 22, 39
Tapestry, 21, 28, 38, 58, *41*
Television, 56, *231*, *236*
Tenements, 45, 60, 64, 68–9, 70, 71, *109*, *168*, *173–4*, *221*, *239*
See also Flats
Terrace housing, 56–9, 59–60, 61, 85, *161*, *163–5*, *185*, *207*
Terraced flats, 65, *218*, *220*
Tester, 21
Thetford, Norfolk, *49*
Thorverton, Devon, *90*
'Tied' cottages, 51
Timber building, 30, 32, 46
    imported, 21, 22
Todmorden, West Yorkshire, *154*, *217*
Toll-house, *154*
Top shop, *169*
Tower, *75*, *76*, *108*, *177*
    house, 27–8, 36, 38, 39, 45, 69, *28*, *29*, *74*, *125*
Treweryn Valley, *230*
Trophy room, *179*
Tydd St. Mary's, Lincolnshire, *114*

Uist, South, Outer Hebrides, *225*
Utensils, domestic, 20

Vanbrugh, Sir John, 48, *135*
Vance roof, 47
Vicarage
See Parsonage house
Vienna, 70
Villa, 49–50, 60, 61, *181–2*
Vitruvius Britannicus (Campbell), 48

Wainscotting, 21, 26, 38, 46, 50, 58, *41*, *150*
Walling, mud, 51, *112*
    turf, 52, *199*, *225*
Wall-paper, 38, 50, 66, *46*
Wardrobe
See Garderobe
Ware, Isaac, *129*
Wash house, 44, 46, 63, 69, *112*, *219*
Washing arrangements, *18–19*, *237*
Water supply, 45, 55, 58, *222*
Watton Priory, East Yorkshire, *32*
'Wealden house', 25, 26, *5*
Well, *111*, *203*
Welwyn Garden City, *233*
Wenham, Little, Suffolk, *3*
Whitby, Yorkshire, *146*, *166*, *168*, *204*
Whitehaven, Cumberland, *161*
Whitewash, 55, 66, *73*
Widecombe in the Moor, Devon, *88–9*
Widmerpool, Nottinghamshire, *122*
Willoughby, Sir Francis, *38*
Wilson, William, 64
Wimbish, Essex, *189*
Windermere, Westmorland, *107*
Window curtains, 38
    seats, 20, *15*
Windows, *61–5*, *98*, *128*, *158*
    sash, 70
Winteringham, Lincolnshire, *132*
Wollaton, Nottinghamshire, *38*
Woodsford Castle, Dorset, *18*

Yard, *167*, *170*, *204*, *208*, *219*
Yarmouth, Great, Norfolk, *29*, *46*
Yaxley, Huntingdonshire, *58*
Yeovil, Somerset, 25
York, 25, 61

208